LET THEM SHOW US THE WAY

Let Them Show Us the Way

Fostering independent learning
in the elementary classroom

ANNE GREEN

Peguis Publishers, Winnipeg, Canada

Printed and bound in Canada by Kromar Printing Limited

95 96 97 98 99 5 4 3 2 1

Canadian Cataloguing in Publication Data

Green, Anne E., 1936-
  Let them show us the way
  Includes bibliographical references.
  ISBN 1-895411-76-9
1. Active learning. 2. Elementary school teaching.
3. Education, Elementary. I. Title
LB1027.23.G74   1995   371.3'9   C95-920173-4

Book and Cover Design: Norman Schmidt
Artwork: Peggy Cowan and Pam Dixon

Peguis Publishers Limited
100-318 McDermot Avenue
Winnipeg, Manitoba
Canada
R3A 0A2

toll free 1-800-667-9673

DEDICATION

To Clarence and Eileen Green, my parents-in-law,
who modeled for their son,
who in turn models for our sons,
"trust yourself as a learner" and "whatever you do,
don't let go of the rope."

In memory of my parents, Walter and Margaret Pettit,
who let me discover the responsibility
that accompanied decision making.

CONTENTS

FOREWORD

This book is written by a true teacher for those who are true teachers and for those who aspire to be true teachers. Anne Green's message comes from a life-long desire to maximize each student's learning every day and to help students become independent learners.

Anne Green was a teacher long before she studied to become one. As a child she was always playing school and living the role of teacher. As a student, prior to university, she felt unfulfilled, less than successful, and couldn't understand why school had to be so uninteresting. Then, she completed her one-year teacher training program in Calgary, and went to a small Alberta town where, determined to make a difference, she began her teaching career.

Education has been in turmoil for many years. In 1967, for example, I wrote a paper about the teaching of science entitled "Traditional vs. Discovery" for one of my university courses. In July 1994 I had occasion to reread that paper and found to my surprise that the ideas I presented then are being talked about today as if they were new. But it has only been in the last few years that some people have started looking at alternative solutions. Anne is one of those people.

Throughout this book, Anne refers to the power of a *community of learners,* as each student shows us the way to his unique way of learning. The community of learners is an environment in which a group of students talk, share, and socialize with an insight that brings about an exceptionally high level of engagement in the learning process.

In *Let Them Show Us the Way*, she talks about students learning how to learn and learning how to function in a community of learners, then shows teachers how they can individualize each child's education. The notion that students, at a very young age, are capable of making decisions according to their needs is still unacceptable to many educators. However, we *know* students can be successful in their search for knowledge when pursuing a passion. The level of independence in each student is just waiting for the opportunity to flourish as the student individualizes his own learning.

This book advocates that learning is for life and life is for learning; life-long learning is a desirous goal and this goal can be met by restructuring the delivery system. The community of learners is the most powerful learning environment I have observed and worked in. Anne has demonstrated this environment, not only in her own classroom, but in the classrooms of many project teachers throughout Alberta. She has the gift of letting students be great and now she gives you, the reader, the opportunity to be part of this shift in the teaching/learning process.

Don Green, Coordinator
Centre for Gifted Education
University of Calgary
August 1995

PREFACE

Little Red Lane

As a young child I could often be found skipping down a lane through a forest of tall trees — tall, at least, to a preschooler — on my way to my grandmother's house. It was a special forest, which loyally guarded the secrets of my forefathers who had labored on this, the family farm. The lane curved by an opening in the trees allowing me (and other travelers) a glimpse of my mother's beautiful vegetable garden, interwoven with flowers like wisps of rainbows after a spring shower. And there my mother would be, hoeing among the rows. She would welcome me, then, with a smile watch as the ever-searching honeybees landed on the garden peas on their way to the sweet peas. I would spend a while reviewing the difference between a weed and an edible plant before my mother invited me to reach where the hoe could not.

It was an enchanting adventure for me as I continued my journey to my grandmother's. Along the little red lane (so christened by my family), I was sure to meet small animals all busily going somewhere.

Soon the lane detoured to the left as if to remind me to count the pigs lounging in the cool mud at the edge of their rickety old pen. Then, the pathway sprung out of the forest onto my grandmother's big green lawns. She lived in the "big house" where my father had spent many years before he married my mother and moved into the little red house on the other side of the forest. There, they farmed, raised four children, and saw to the needs of my grandmother in the "big house."

I raced across the yard to find the door to the house ajar and "Gama" waiting for me. Not even the news on the radio stopped us from heading straight to the sunroom with the golden drapes and big wicker rocking chair. We shared storybooks as we rocked to new and exotic places all around the world.

That was truly a magical time, which came to an end the day Gama got a headache and fell asleep. I began school soon after — at the one-room schoolhouse at the far end of my father's field. This new experience didn't build onto my first encounters with authors and books. The books at school had three leading characters called Dick, Jane, and Sally who spent their entire time running, jumping, or playing. You might say I felt a loss of paradise at a very early age.

* * *

My quest, as I become one with *this* book, is not to regain that magical time for myself, but to help you understand children and learning and how school can be a continuation of those formative years — years that are the world for each child. It is a world not to be judged or changed, for it is in this world children begin to shape themselves — with strengths and weaknesses, passions, questions, and fears.

I envision our schools, with warm nurturing environments, as the next rocking chair, where children may continue their learning journey in a place where everyone's contributions are needed and valued; where each child recalls experiences from his own little red lane and stretches his spontaneous thinking while building on the ideas of a classmate; where personal projects spring up around the learning; where each child naturally weaves experiences with good literature as learning skips in many directions.

As a facilitator, learner, and teacher in both kindergarten and first-grade classrooms for many years, I have had the privilege of observing children as they continue *their* learning journey within a community of learners.

This book is based on my experiences as a participant in a community of learners involving children, parents, and colleagues. I have learned, as I hope you will, that for students to become involved in risk-taking and decision making, the structure of the classroom must be hidden. The coveted teaching skill is observation. Observation is something I practice mainly from the edge of the learning community, for it reveals insights that I come to understand as I embark on reflective writing, talk with my colleagues, and read books written by leading people in the field of education who promote integration, program continuity, differentiation, child-centered classrooms, portfolio assessment, and parents in partnership. All these work in concert to form the rudder of a holistic learning environment that is necessary if our children are to become independent thinkers.

This book, then, is about children stretching their thinking as they interact, talk, write, and read while making their learning personal and meaningful within a community of learners. It is my aim to leave you, not with a recipe, but energized to play host to your own community of learners.

ACKNOWLEDGMENTS

I am grateful to the many people who assisted and supported me on my journey. I want to say a special thank you to the following:

- the children, who will meet the year 2000 with confidence

- parents, as they trust their children as learners

- the community members who spent time sharing their expertise for children

- a support staff for their support and smiles of confidence. Special mention goes to Lorraine Debnam for her continuous awareness of the children's and my needs; to Judy Powell who, in appreciation of learning as a process, shared as she transcribed the students' invented spellings; to Judy Foster who, prior to me having the courage to sit down at a computer, typed as I talked.

- a custodial staff who always had a minute to discuss a better arrangement of our classroom space

- Inez Schofield, who joined the class, contributing to the learning as she quietly listened to the wonderful ideas and Connie Johnston, who wrote poetry. I would arrive in the morning to find her taking a moment from her busy schedule to share her writing with the children.

- my colleagues, for their honesty. They did not just accept the concept of the community of learners, but continually questioned whether it did what it appeared to do. They listened, even when I forgot to exchange pleasantries in my excitement to share another wonderful book I had just read about children and learning and parents as partners.

- Lorretta Stabler for asking the right question at the right time, causing me to explore concepts either in greater detail or in a different direction

◆ Shirley Taylor, my sister, and a teacher who loved every word I wrote

◆ beginning teachers for their enthusiasm, which I find so contagious. They always made me feel so happy and important even though I was learning just as they were.

◆ Dr. Carl Braun, who helped me to trust myself as a learner when I returned to my studies following a period of time in the classroom, being a mom, and reading as an independent learner; Dr. Michael Lupart, who has the gift of surprise and is always thrilled to learn new ideas; Dr. Bill Washburn and Mary Frampton, who became my mentors when I spent a summer at the Calgary Writing Project internalizing the concept that writing is the secret to learning

◆ the consultants, university professors, practicum students, teachers, and parents from all parts of Alberta, the Department of Education, as well as out-of-province visitors from British Columbia, Ontario, Montana, and Moscow — your questions and letters helped me build onto my learning

◆ the people at the Centre for Gifted Education, University of Calgary, who, under the direction of Dr. Judy Lupart, shared their books, ideas, and philosophies on how kids learn

◆ Don Green, my colleague, friend, and husband who continues to help me understand that "gifted education" is happening when children use their own experiences and questions to bring meaning to theory, a concept that richly became hands-on as we raised our two sons. He was my principal during the growing awareness of the paradigm shift in education, and enhanced my confidence in writing to learn by placing a lap-top computer under the Christmas tree.

EDITOR'S NOTE

One of the dilemmas facing today's editor is that of retaining writing clarity while ensuring gender balance. This relates specifically to the use of the personal pronouns he/she, him/her, himself/herself, and so on. Using both forms in all cases makes for particularly awkward reading. In this book, we have chosen to use masculine pronouns in reference to students and feminine pronouns in reference to teachers. We assure the reader that no affront is intended in any way.

Introduction
THE QUEST

The real voyage of discovery consists not in seeking new landscapes but in having new eyes.

– Marcel Proust, *The Maxims of Marcel Proust*

I once heard someone say, "Our education of the past was not wrong, but please let us not remain there." We are grateful that our doctors and dentists are no longer practicing as they were in the 1940s and 1950s. In 1958 my father, diagnosed with heart disease, knew he faced a shortened life and died within four years of the diagnosis. Today he would have enjoyed extended life because changes in the field of medicine better suit individual needs as theory and practice combine to make improvements. Should it be any different for education?

BEGINNINGS

When I began teaching, my only source of professional reading was the big thick teacher guidebooks, one for each subject. I had memorized Bloom's Taxonomy at university but somehow left that knowledge on the test paper I had handed in for the sole purpose of getting a passing grade. I would return from teachers' meetings and conventions on Monday mornings with an approach or an activity for all of the students. The whole staff would be energized to make a difference; however, it wasn't long before many of us began checking the number of pages left in the sets of readers and spelling and phonics workbooks and counted the hours till Friday afternoon, when we and the children could be creative. It would be then that the children would excitedly pull me along rather than me push and coax them with extrinsic motivations such as special favors and gold stars.

My quest really began, though, the year, as the new member of the staff, I was given young students who were "at risk." I soon discovered that learning with these children was a great privilege. They went about their learning in a wealth of interesting ways, once we dutifully completed the required workbooks together. They were so free and creative. They were honest about what they didn't want to do and I learned that they were right about how they could learn in different ways. It was then that I truly began to search for ways to help students help themselves. I wanted to understand about children and learning as they take a leading role in their own education. I wanted to honor their learning strengths and special abilities. And, I wanted to understand the process of theory and practice coming together into a meaningful context in the classroom.

During those early years I also taught older students. I often spent my evenings writing pages of notes in subjects such as social studies, transferring the notes to the chalkboard the next day for everyone to copy and learn for the test. One young man, I remember, was always reading a book. He would half-heartedly write a little then return to his book. That was when I began to negotiate with students, saying things like, "Read this, then make note of anything you are not familiar with. Remember, you must make an 80 percent test score." I later learned that the student who was always reading books could read social sciences texts at a university level.

I was also fortunate to spend time learning with children in a far northern community. I learned to step back as these young problem solvers with meaningful life skills dropped into my class-room for a few days a week. They were able to naturally control their learning as they shared their experiences and stories. The illustrations, talk, and writing became the material that brought the curriculum to life. Not surprisingly, the stacks of readers, spellers, and phonics books slept on the shelf while the children demonstrated their understanding of the world around them. This, as I think back, was truly an inclusive classroom[1] of children building onto their personal ideas while building onto one anoth-er's ideas and experiences. In this classroom, I came to under-stand that what I at one time would have taken to be chaos was actually children highly engaged in the learning process as they exitedly and freely talked, role-played, and created from their real world. I could, for the first time, well identify with the words of Sylvia Ashton-Warner (1986,93):

> Yet I'm a disciplinarian. It's just that I like the lid off. I like seeing what's there. I like unpredictability and gaiety and interesting people, however small, and funny things happen-ing and wild things happening and sweet, and everything that life is, uncovered. I hate covers of any kind. I like the true form of living, even in school. I'm in love with the organic shape...I understand, I understand, but communica-tion and creativity are abler teachers than a foot.

Then my teaching journey followed a challenging path with colleagues in a southern school. We were inspired by a principal who had a vision of making a difference for students in our

---

[1] The inclusive classroom is one in which education is inclusive. It is "the merger of special and regular education into a unified educational system" (Andrews and Lupart 1993). The community of learners is one way to help *all* children meet their learning needs in the regular classroom. As they work, they naturally show the teacher who is independent, who works well with a partner or in a small group, and who needs direct instruction. Children with special needs, talents, and understandings were not separated from the other children in my northern classroom.

school. Our journey involved living our philosophy each day, which basically was an extension of the community school logo, "Everyone a teacher, everyone a learner." Donald Treffinger, George Betts, Sally Patton, to name a few, were to become our mentors as we began to break new ground.

I spent summers at the university listening to Merron Chorny and reading James Britton. I felt like I had wings as they shared: "Talk is an established instrument for developing classroom communities in which teachers and students can collaborate to learn from and with each other" (Chorny 1988, 2). I learned of Vygotsky and how he views learning as a social process that emphasizes dialoguing about tasks that are relevant to the learner's life and how he believes children should be taught to read and write in the same way they learn to speak.

I built onto the importance of good literature in children's learning — they have to enjoy the stories and meet characters they can dream with, identify with, worship, worry with, and solve problems with.

I embraced the work of Dr. Howard Gardner and his theory of multiple intelligences — linguistic, logical-mathematical, spatial, musical, bodily-kinesthetic, interpersonal, and intrapersonal — and learned to look at each child as unique in his learning style.

I attended the Calgary Writing Project and experienced what it meant to use writing as a tool to learn, to have a voice with fellow students and instructors, and to see my first article published in an educational magazine. I was introduce to the writings of Donald Graves and Lucy McCormick Calkins whose books have become an intregal part of my professional library. And it was at about this time that, as a student, I came to understand what Calkins (1994, 283) meant when she said: "Unless children are conscious of an author's technique when they read, it is hard to imagine that they will deliberately borrow these techniques when they write." Calkins made me realize how important it is to read lots of good literature to students to model techniques for writing, as well as for enjoyment, and to give them the opportunity to comment on the way an author begins a story, brings a character to life, and so on.

The thrill of actually being a part of a community of learners in university happened one summer when I spent a few weeks in a class about philosophy for children. Our professor, George Ghanotakis, modeled, to its ultimate, the role of a facilitator, as together the class formed a community of learners and discovered: "It is only the intellectual give-and-take of conversation that one has with one's peers that can stimulate reflection" (Lipman et al. 1980, 211). Back in my own classroom, I began to see children — even those in first grade — reflect on what was being discussed, tie it to their own experiences, and expand their thinking.

I found myself reading just one more chapter from one of my professional books while I watched my sons' basketball games or rodeo-roping competitions. I learned that we can do more than one thing at a time — something I respect when students in my class are writing and listening at the same time.

UNDERSTANDING THE RESEARCH

My learning quest was motivated by one question: How do I step back and let the children find the answers yet feel secure that what is happening in my classroom is educationally sound? I realized that my role as participant/observer would be enhanced if I understood the research and the work of master teachers. The following major areas guided the focus of my quest:

◆ the philosophy of whole language and its implications for writing to learn

◆ writing as a process and the understanding that writing, like talking, is developmental

◆ talk, where children are participants, not just listeners

◆ writing as a tool to learn across the curriculum

◆ storying (bringing one's world to the conversation or to the page)

◆ spelling as a process from temporary to conventional

◆ literature that supports the learning process

◆ questioning techniques

◆ learning styles beyond visual, auditory, and kinesthetic

◆ teaching styles

◆ evaluation/portfolio assessment

Theory and practice must come together if we are to agree on a paradigm that will maximize student learning. It is the responsibility of each teacher to become increasingly involved in the practice of research within the classroom environment as we revisit how students learn. The students take much more of a leading role if we provide the opportunity in a meaningful way (Goswami and Stillman 1987). As Margaret Donaldson (1978, 118) says: "...we enjoy best and engage most readily in activities which we *experience as freely chosen. We do not like being controlled, we like controlling ourselves.*"

CHAPTER OVERVIEWS

In *Let Them Show Us the Way*, I share my experiences and learning, while I am an integral part of a community of learners in the classroom. I share the specialness of that nurturing environment where students take ownership for their learning as they become instrumental in meeting their own needs. I, as the learning teacher in that environment, see my role as helping students to help themselves.

In chapter 1, I introduce the reader to a community of learners in action and talk about *learning energy*, which is determined by how each member sees himself within the community and is directly proportional to how each member sees himself as having choice. In chapter 2, I celebrate the child-centered classroom, where children's passions and storying, supported by good literature, give personal meaning to new learning challenges. Chapter

3 focuses on how to get started; this is not a recipe, rather, an explanation of what a teacher does in a community of learners so that her actions and questions invite the students to take ownership for their learning. I also discuss how children take control of their learning as they use communication skills (for example, talking and writing) as tools for learning.

In chapter 4, I talk about how themes — designed to encourage the six levels of thinking as outlined in Bloom's Taxonomy — can facilitate students as they make choices and decisions about their learning. Chapter 5 invites readers to read about children bonding with the writing of authors as they make decisions about their learning. In chapter 6, I use science fair projects to demonstrate how children develop a real interest in learning, then mediate their learning as they talk, construct, illustrate, and write to make sense of their hypotheses. The process grows in new directions as they seek books to verify and support their ideas and premises. In chapter 7, students in the community of learners demonstrate the lively process of incorporating divergent thinking with serious communication as they create and produce plays and songs with and for an audience. The concern about evaluation and how assessment should take place is discussed in chapter 8. Parent/teacher conferences help us understand a child's zone of proximal development.

As parents become caught up in the excitement of the changes in education, they become mentors and partners. In chapter 9, they join the community of learners and sit in the circle to chat, read, write, listen, and observe students taking charge of their learning. In chapter 10, I discuss the important role that the school administrator plays, not only by providing leadership, but also by empowering the staff so that they might empower the students. Finally, I conclude with a story about how recognition of a student's unique way of learning, supported by the community of learners, encourages self-directed learning.

1
A COMMUNITY
OF LEARNERS:
A Snake Lands in a
Banana Peel

The head goose — the leader of the V —
suddenly veered out, leaving a vacancy
which was promptly filled by the bird behind.

The former leader then flew alongside,
the formation continued growing wide —
and he found a place at the back of the line.
They never missed a beat.

– R.D. Stomberg, *The Goose*

I would like to share with you the pulse of my classroom — the talking, thinking, questioning, squigglyness,[1] and the discovering. The pulse is perpetuated within the inner sanctity of my community of learners. It is a classroom where energy ebbs and flows in direct proportion to how each student sees himself as having choice.

How, then, may our students see themselves as having choice in the classroom? I believe the key is through a way of thinking about thinking. Frank Smith (1990) calls this *commonplace thinking*. It occurs naturally all day, every day, and must be as welcome in the classroom as it is outside of school. In this chapter, I unfold a nurturing environment, where commonplace thinking is ongoing in every subject and flows from the students'

---

[1] Squigglyness is that period when a student is just about ready to move to the next stage of development and learning. For parents and teachers, it is a time to stand back — even when it appears nothing is getting done — and let the student discover for himself. Self-confidence is the greatest gift we can give a child.

everyday interests and passions. It is instrumental in webbing their experiences with the curriculum as it is powered by the interaction within a community of learners. In such an environment children take charge of their learning, as their strengths and gifts rise to their potential. From Vygotsky (1978) we learn that what a child can do in cooperation with adults and peers today, he can do alone tomorrow. Thus, as children sense that their thinking is needed and valued daily in the school setting they come to trust themselves as learners. They enjoy their discoveries, learn to make decisions, and see themselves as having a voice.

CREATING THE ENVIRONMENT

In this classroom, the students and I create an environment in which a community of learners can experience learning. Or maybe it is the community of learners experiencing learning that creates the environment.

Here, the children's desks, or home base (as they call it), are arranged in a circle, leaving a wonderful free area in the center for impromptu mime, plays, dance, and groups gathering to hear a story, song, or poem woven into the learning (see figure 1.1). The outer edge of the classroom accommodates painting, music, books, manipulatives, children's projects, and small groups of students, parents, and the teacher — all of whom can slip in and out of the center to mediate or join the ongoing learning.

Within this community of learners, everyone is expected to do the following:

◆ Refrain from stepping on anyone else's words. Teachers and parents, in particular, must be aware that as children interact socially, adding their story versions and asking questions, the narrative invariably improves. Often what adults think of as interruptions actually give wings to the stories.

Figure 1.1: An example of the physical arrangement of a classroom.

◆ Build onto one another's ideas and accept all ideas as a part of the thinking that is responsible for webbing the rich and welcome everyday knowledge with the school knowledge, and vice versa.

◆ Use space wisely.

◆ Stay on task.

◆ Share as needed with a peer or an adult in the room after asking politely if that person can spare a minute.

◆ Assemble at home base to share works-in-progress. Everyone is welcome to continue writing; however, out of respect for those wishing to share, side conversation is not welcome.

◆ Give whole class attention when there is a teacher lesson or a guest speaker.

◆ Give whole class attention when a peer is celebrating his published work. This is a time when a typed copy, modeling the conventions of language, has been handed to everyone for reading and imaging. (Imaging is a strategy where students draw what is happening in the story.) This is followed by the author reading his work aloud and asking for any questions or comments. All children read in some fashion and comprehension is never a problem. During questions and comments, the author often images his meaning on the chalkboard. This becomes an excellent way for teachers to see the differentiated learning that occurs naturally in the classroom.

◆ Understand that when asked to *focus* as a whole class there will be strategies, skills, stories read, or information shared in context with the ongoing learning. (This is a time when the teacher takes advantage of the "teachable moments.")

◆ Take advantage of one-to-one mini-lessons. During these lessons, it is important to practice listening, wondering, and questioning with the student. This can be a time of growth and self-discovery, and often a student just needs encouragement to use his own ideas to solve a problem.

The Catalysts

The catalysts in this community are

◆ a learning teacher who supports independent thinking by listening to students and ensures the growth of ideas by asking questions, not dispensing information

◆ a philosophy that supports the belief that learning becomes a personal discovery as it branches from commonplace thinking across the curriculum

◆ quality literature, which becomes a resource for children as they build upon interests and passions

◆ parents as partners in learning

The three scenarios that follow are about children involved in learning as it diverges within a community of learners.

A SNAKE LANDS IN A BANANA PEEL

The theme, Reptiles and Amphibians, was supporting the present high interest of the classroom. Amelia, who had previously shared her dislike for snakes and didn't want to write about them, was wandering about the room one February morning with a frown on her tiny brow.

Aware of her visual learning style, I suggested she draw a few big circles on the chalkboard so that she might sequentially map the images for her story, which may or may not have a snake in it. Amelia began to illustrate her story. Then, on her own, she transferred her concrete images into words in her notebook, using her temporary spelling. Later the children assembled to share their stories-in-progress. When it was Amelia's turn to read, everyone, familiar with one another's passion areas, was listening, ready to support. However, Amelia, who had illustrated and written about princesses since she had first joined the community of learners in September, hadn't written about princesses. Imagine our surprise when she read us a snake story. This is what happened.

AMELIA (*Reading her story*): A man was walking in the forest. He came to a snake. He picked it up and swung the snake around and around, throwing it into a banana peel. A monkey ate it. The end. (*Pauses*) Any questions or comments?

MALCOLM: I don't understand. If the monkey just bit the snake's tail, the snake would just grow another one. He wouldn't be dead.

AMELIA: Well that's how I got rid of the snake in my story. (Note: As the author, it is Amelia's privilege to determine the outcome of her story. This privilege gives an author a wonderful sense of control.)

ANDY: I don't understand how a snake could fit in a banana peel. He would hang out and the monkey would see him.

MATHIAS (*Running back from the reptile center with a book*): Amelia, I want to build onto what Andy said. Here is a snake that could fit into a banana peel. It is called the Northern Red-bellied Snake. Right, Malcolm? (*Mathias and Malcolm are continually consulting references about snakes. Sharing such information with their classmates makes everyone aware that nonfiction gives credibility to fiction stories.*)

KENNY: I like how the man swung the snake over his head. (*He jumps up to act out the way he envisioned the action in Amelia's story — much to the delight of the students.*)

AMELIA (*Smiling*): Yes, that's what he did.

I then noticed that the book Mathias was referring to had a foreword written by Barbara Froom (1972), a leading authority on snakes. As I read from the foreword, Amelia was amazed to learn that when Barbara was three she had touched a huge python; from then on she begged her mother for a pet snake. Her mother compromised by stuffing two of Barbara's long stockings and sewing them together, then painting a face on one end and making a little forked tongue out of pieces of red wool. Barbara went on to say: "I soon obtained a beautiful little garter snake about sixteen inches long, whom I named Bijou because of his jewel-like appearance. He had vivid yellow and black coloring and huge amber eyes." From this, Amelia learned that girls can have a deep interest in snakes. Barbara went on to tell about her snakes living together and of how a ten-year-old boy who saw her pets commented that if humans could get along together and share their territory like these different species of snakes, there wouldn't be any wars.

Amelia and the community of learners expanded and built upon their fund of knowledge. We looked at forewords in other books and the richness of language used by authors writing non-fiction stories (for example, "jewel-like appearance"). And, I had found that precious, teachable time to build onto the learning.

One of the student's parents and her little sister had joined us in the classroom that morning. The father, Mr. Lalonde, was impressed with the children's spontaneity as they used language to enhance learning. After listening to Amelia's story and the dialogue that followed, he reflected, "You have to see it to believe what a community of learners can do with a story from one of its members."

Mrs. Lalonde and three-year-old Rosie often sat in my classroom writing stories. One day, Mrs. Lalonde and Rosie captivated the children's attention when they shared their stories (figures 1.2 and 1.3). In *The Mule Deer's Ballet*, the analogy of the mule deer to a ballet sparked questions, more stories, and children dancing as they demonstrated their sense of ballet dancing. It was break time and everyone was getting a snack. I slipped Tchaikovsky's *Chinese Dance* on the record player. (Classical music is yet another support for learning.) Malcolm, spontaneously swaying to the music, informed everyone, "Snakes can do ballet." On that note we broke for recess.

The Mule Deer's Ballet

The meadow was silent. The soft deep snow glistened with the bright sunlight. Spring was near - chirping and chattering like the birds along the river. Our horses froze mid-stride. Sidekick, the eager border collie, had bounded off into the brushes.

Suddenly the willow started to vibrate and quiver. The horses hearts started to beat faster. So did mine.

CRASH!!!!!

Like cymbals in an orchestra the lead dancers broke through the woods. Leaping and bounding in all directions, they numbered close to 50. The choreography was unbelievable, - the musical score provided by Mother Nature. The dancers circled our horses. We waited breathlessly for what would happen next. The largest dancer, resplendent in a coat of brilliant bronze with immaculate white socks and tail, bounded directly towards us. He froze in the air and spun about- leaping off the meadow's stage and through the woods. The remaining dancers took this as a final cue to exit - and they departed in all directions.

We stayed rooted to our spot, finally daring to breath. The horses snorted and stamped the snow, anxious to join in the fun. The dancers - why they were gone - vanished as quickly as they had appeared. But their magic will stay with me for the rest of my life. What a special treat- a mule deer's ballet!!!

Figure 1.2: Through this story, written by the mother of one of the students, the children were introduced to similes in the natural talk and sharing in the community of learners.

Figure 1.3: Three-year-old Rosie wrote this story when she joined the community of learners. She was naturally writing to learn.

The Hidden Curriculum

Mr. Lalonde came back to school a few days later and together we shared about the hidden curriculum being addressed in a meaningful context. We talked about how

◆ the author (Amelia) was making the alphabet work for her, rather than working to learn the alphabet

◆ students were asking questions, demonstrating comprehension

◆ the author was naturally defending and justifying her story

◆ children were balancing logic with creativity

◆ students were checking sources to help confirm an idea

◆ students were building on one another's ideas

◆ their spontaneous dialogue revealed ownership for learning

◆ social skills were being lived, not being taught

Then he showed me a rhyming poem he had written (see figure 1.4). He shyly mentioned that I could read this to the class if I would like. I think he wanted to join his family of writers (see page 14). I asked him to come to the classroom and read the poem, and told him we could initiate a fun time with rhyme. He left with assurance that learning in this setting is rich and meaningful, and that spelling, which was a concern and had motivated his presence in the classroom, is only one piece of the process for his daughter Leigh as she embarks on her learning journey (see figure 1.5).

I find that learning rarely misses a beat as everyone, myself included, knows when it is time to take the lead within the community of learners.

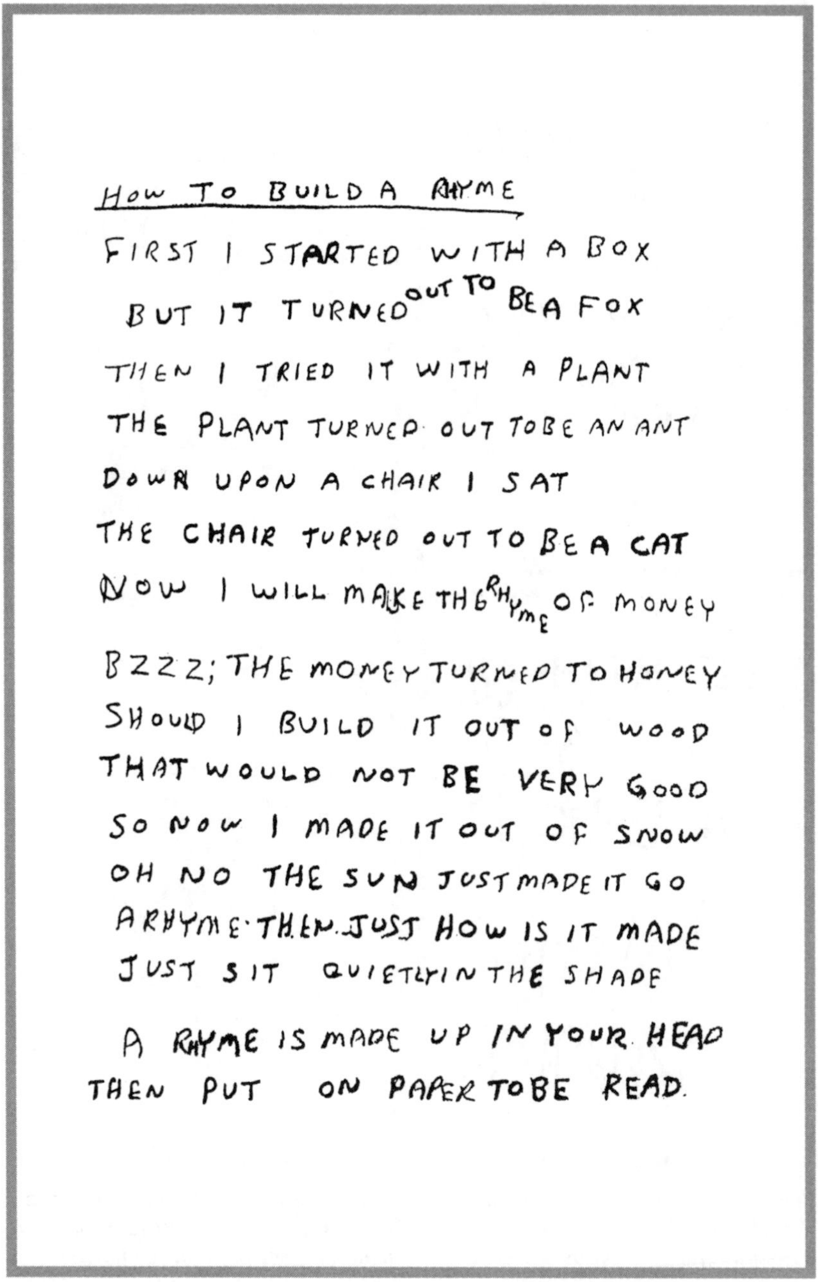

<u>HOW TO BUILD A RHYME</u>

FIRST I STARTED WITH A BOX

BUT IT TURNED OUT TO BE A FOX

THEN I TRIED IT WITH A PLANT

THE PLANT TURNED OUT TO BE AN ANT

DOWN UPON A CHAIR I SAT

THE CHAIR TURNED OUT TO BE A CAT

NOW I WILL MAKE THE RHYME OF MONEY

BZZZ; THE MONEY TURNED TO HONEY

SHOULD I BUILD IT OUT OF WOOD

THAT WOULD NOT BE VERY GOOD

SO NOW I MADE IT OUT OF SNOW

OH NO THE SUN JUST MADE IT GO

A RHYME THEN JUST HOW IS IT MADE

JUST SIT QUIETLY IN THE SHADE

A RHYME IS MADE UP IN YOUR HEAD

THEN PUT ON PAPER TO BE READ.

Figure 1.4: How to Build a Rhyme *was written by the father of one of the students. He brought the poem to school to share with the grade-one class.*

1. IMy momms HorsES IS NAD Athos My HorSES iS NAD HANe

2. SI LOVE HANe He LOVE me

3. 4I Wet On to A tr A LRed Weth My Hors

4. My HoSe SPot I FLAIL AF R My Horse R Awh I KAD My Hors K BAK I ROD D mo BT I Wet ABAN I SAW A BAY Br

Figure 1.5: (a) Leigh, a grade-one student, experiments to find out how the alphabet will help her save her stories. She is sounding and using phonics in a meaningful context as she writes, motivated by her passion for horses.

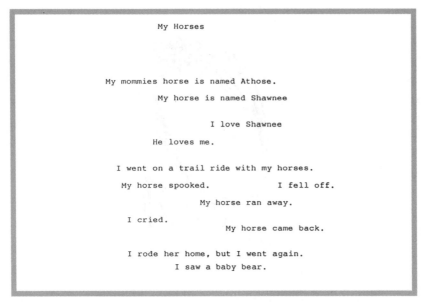

```
                        My Horses



        My mommies horse is named Athose.
              My horse is named Shawnee

                    I love Shawnee
              He loves me.

        I went on a trail ride with my horses.
        My horse spooked.              I fell off.
                      My horse ran away.
            I cried.
                        My horse came back.

          I rode her home, but I went again.
                I saw a baby bear.
```

Figure 1.5 (cont'd): (b) Leigh's story, using conventional spelling.

WHY DO BABIES CRY? WHY DO PEOPLE CRY?

Meet Marni. She is building upon her experiences as she stretches her thinking while meeting her learning needs (see figure 1.6).

Involved in an individual project, she stopped to share a photograph of her little sister crying. Then she announced that her question for her project was, "Why do little sisters cry?" She explained, "The reason is that she wants her Baba." During the course of the conversation within the community others suggested that Marni's little sister may be uncomfortable due to wet pants, may be frightened, or may be lonely. One member of the class, as she wove in her experiences, said that her eyes watered when she stood too close to her mother when she was peeling an onion. Another shared that his grandfather's eyes watered in cold air. One boy, who usually enjoyed listening, blurted out that his grandfather and he were wondering if the clouds were crying when it rained. Emily, looking up from her writing, emphasized that her mother once said that she cried crocodile tears when

Figure 1.6: Marni drew a picture of herself and proudly showed it to her classmates as her project took shape — an indication she knows she can make a difference and is a part of the learning community.

she didn't get her own way. That led to a sophisticated chat about crocodiles. As Britton (1992,157) writes: "It is the stories that will spread as they merge with the interests of the children, sparking off inquiries, investigations, expeditions, projects, and even at times culminating in a display of work."

I decided that this was an opportune time to read stories of celebrated authors to help this rich, divergent thinking in a direction somewhat closer to Marni's intent. Mordicai Gerstein's *The Gigantic Baby,* about a new baby sister who, while crying nonstop, grows too big for the house, is an example of a literary exaggeration. Gerstein shares with his readers that often "it's a little laughter that is needed to make things right again." However, after hearing *Go and Hush the Baby* by Betsy Byars, and Frieda Wishinsky's *Oonga Boonga*, Marni was convinced that her original solution — a crying baby needs a bottle — was a possible answer to her question.

In each of the stories we read, an older child sang and told stories to help with a crying sibling. Marni was motivated to learn songs and stories and also to write her own to entertain her little sister.

Someone suggested that the delightful sounds in *Oonga Boonga* are used by babies as they become tellers of stories. This helped a few children, including Marni, understand that sounding and using temporary spelling are natural for beginning writers of stories.

Robert Munsch's *Show and Tell* led to a special visit one morning from Marni's mother and her baby sister. Marni's mother and the baby sat among the children while they continued to write. As some shared their exciting stories scripted in all earnest with temporary spelling and I made a few comments, Marni's mother began to relax and to enjoy the stories as the children wrote to learn. We chatted about the parallel between babies beginning to talk and children beginning to write as they transfer their talk to writing. We talked about how the children were drawing and sounding (a powerful use of meaningful phonics) as they saved their stories onto the paper. It all seemed a natural extension of thinking to use one's mouth to discover that magical process of converting speech to print. I explained to Marni's mother that I encourage the children to let the sounds they hear as they make them in their mouths flow down their arms, down their pencils, and onto the paper. Later, I gave her a copy of Judith Newman's book *The Craft of Children's Writing*. In it, Newman explains how to encourage children to write independently, using their own temporary spelling methods.

Marni's thinking was stretched as she chatted with her peers and identified with story characters who were busy solving the challenges of a crying baby. She decided to change the question for her project to "Why do people cry?" She researched the mysteries of tear ducts and asked questions such as, "Why do tears taste salty?" Following a visit to the doctor's office with her mother and little sister, Marni came to school with pamphlets on how to care for eyes. She was experiencing the never-ending thrill of learning, as the wondering and questioning led to more wondering and questioning. Marni was learning to take advantage of her world in and out of school as she naturally built onto her experience.

We discovered and shared many exciting books about tears. Marni's classmates, while continuing their own chosen projects, were motivated to expand their perception of tears. In *The Wizard's Tears*, authors Maxine Kumin and Anne Sexton disclose a special wizard power — the tears induced by peeling an onion can bring rain in a drought-stricken area. Emily loved Andre François' words and drawing in *Crocodile Tears*, especially the French captions, as she was interested in learning to speak French. Laura suddenly felt that she understood why Alice in *Alice in Wonderland* found her lake of tears salty. *The Sad Story of Veronica Who Played the Violin*, by David McKee, caused Barry, who had been studying the violin since he was four, to giggle with a sparkle in his eye and wonder if he could play music so sad that people would cause a flood with their tears.

The child's interests create, for himself and for the community, a mushrooming of learning for learning's sake. Stories and poetry find their way into the community of learners daily, not to motivate a contrived lesson, but to help the children help themselves build onto perceptions of their personal world and, in turn, to mediate formal learning. Vygotsky (Moll 1990,10) emphasized: "It is through the use of everyday concepts that children make sense of the definitions and explanations of scientific concepts; everyday concepts provide the living knowledge for the development of scientific concepts." He goes on to say: "...everyday concepts also become dependent on, are mediated and transformed by the scientific concepts."

Marni's wonderings about her crying sister "blazed the trail" for herself and her peers to include the experiences of well-known authors as they made learning personal and meaningful. The synthesizing of ideas in the social setting of the community of learners helped Marni understand scientific concepts as well as transfer her learning to her everyday challenges by reading and writing stories for her little sister.

Marni was encouraged, within the community of learners, to build an interest into a sophisticated study. This interest became the vehicle for her to hook into reading, writing, illustrating, talking, and organizing as she made decisions about her learning. She built onto the interests and experiences from her world.

In my experience, I have found Vygotsky's zone of proximal development increases naturally as children weave their authentic home learning with the demands of school learning. The development is stretched and enriched as I seize those opportune moments within the community of learners, to encourage a child to become one with the world of books.

MY DOG GOBBLES HIS FOOD DOWN

Jamal is a quiet, deep-thinking little boy with a warm, inviting smile and a look about him that says "I know, but the time to share isn't yet" as he puts his hands in his pockets and watches.

One morning Jamal, as presenting author, passed out copies of his first published story to all of his peers. Everyone read and imaged the story, some asking him for help. Then Jamal was invited to read his story aloud.

In the following conversations, the children used their experiences to reflect, analyze, and hypothesize while building deeper understanding. (Note the weaving of curriculum to support the learning.)

JAMAL (*Reading his story*): I fed my dog. He gobbled his food down. (*Looks up to see Sandbo's hand waving impatiently. Then, with great importance*) Sandbo?

SANDBO: Don't dogs gobble their food up?

JAMAL: My dog gobbled his food down into his stomach. (*He goes to the chalkboard and draws a diagram.*) Here's the windpipe and the lungs. The windpipe is shut off. The food goes down this tube to the stomach. My dog eats Kiblets. Here are the Kiblets going down. (See figure 1.7.)

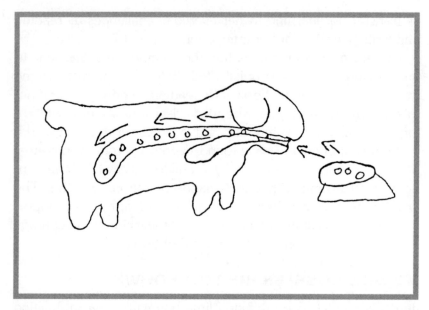

Figure 1.7: Jamal uses arrows to show how food goes into the stomach of his dog.

Everyone was very quiet. Some of the children began copying Jamal's diagram onto their copy of his story. Jamal had captivated his audience but no chat seemed to be forthcoming. It appeared to be a moment where I might help Sandbo develop his point of view (the trick of facilitating is to pick up on those quiet little comments).

MRS. GREEN: Where are the Kiblets to begin with, Jamal?

JAMAL: In the dog's dish.

MRS. GREEN: Does Sandbo have a point, in that the dog has to get the Kiblets up from the dish?

JAMAL (*He draws arrows to show the process.*): Yes. He has to pick the Kiblets up from his dish before they can go down the tube to his stomach. (*Sandbo smiles.*)

All ideas are welcome and invaluable to the learning. What might seem like an insignificant comment may be the seed of a great idea that spurs on the talk. Reciprocal teaching was naturally incorporated as Jamal took the chalk and further explained his ideas using diagrams that helped his classmates with visual learning styles. Figure 1.7 shows the addition of the arrows.

MRS. GREEN: What is that tube called?

That question led to further class discussion about the esophagus and the trachea. The lessons about lungs and breathing that had previously been discussed by the whole class were being reviewed in detail. The review took place naturally in a meaningful context as Jamal shared his knowledge and interest in windpipes, while incorporating his home world with his school world.

LISA: Jamal, my dog loves Kiblets, too.
(*Jamal smiles, then acknowledges Keegan.*)

KEEGAN: What color and what kind is your dog?

JAMAL: He is just brown.

KEEGAN (*Always one to delve logically into a discussion, he runs over to the pictures in a pocket at the theme center. The theme is about dogs.*): Jamal, does your dog look like this brown dog?

There was rich discussion about kinds of dogs as the students viewed the many pictures of dogs Keegan held up, one at a time.

As the students completed their individual diagrams of Jamal's dog eating Kiblets, Sandbo, still making his point, was busy labeling the journey of the Kiblets on the diagram at the chalkboard. Three or four children joined him to figure out how to spell "up" and "down" (see figure 1.8).

JAMAL: Good idea, Sandbo.

Figure 1.8: Sandbo added the words "down" and "up" to Jamal's diagram to help his classmates with visual learning styles.

Jamal's dad happened to be in the classroom. As Jamal returned to his desk from the chalkboard he and his father began chatting intently. I learned later that they were making plans to build a model to show how the windpipe can be shut off. This was to become Jamal's focus for his science fair project. (Jamal spent weekends with his father as he has two families. This would be something special and meaningful for he and his father to pursue together.)

I encouraged everyone to label their individual diagrams. Word drill and modeling of conventional spelling were happening naturally. I also invited the class to enjoy Dayal Kaur Khalsa's story *I Want a Dog*. It is about a young girl who demonstrates how she would take responsibility for the care of a dog if her parents would consent to having one. Good literature helped the entire class to expand on the care of dogs. It modeled a story line with a beginning, several problems, and innovative ways to solve the problems. The story lent itself to further discussions of how authors weave fact with fiction to make a story believable.

* * *

Figure 1.9: Kyla's sketch of her community of learners.

In my classroom, the structure, though hidden, is modeled and practiced within the learning context; it is the framework within which we operate as a community of learners.

Amelia, Marni, and Jamal shared their thinking with their community of learners and trusted themselves as learners while experiencing their personal ideas taking new shape. They truly showed us the way!

2
THE CHILD-CENTERED CLASSROOM:
Another Story in My Toque*

> "Remember only this one thing," said Beaver. "The stories people tell
> have a way of taking care of them. And learn to give them away where
> they are needed. Sometimes a person needs a story more than food to
> stay alive. That is why we put these stories in each other's memory.
> This is how people care for themselves."
>
> – Barry Lopez, *Crow and Weasel*

A colleague recently said to me, "Children are very self-centered these days and doing whatever they want in child-centered classrooms is not going to help. They have to be told." A parent once told me, "Too much attention is damaging, making it difficult for children to outgrow their infantile self-centeredness. They are overindulged, as every whim is deemed necessary to give them experience. At home, everything from what to wear, ready-made toys, planned out-of-school lessons, television, home videos, and computer games have slipped in to control the decision making. At school, to further add to the dilemma, the classrooms are becoming child-centered where everyone can do whatever they wish."

Certainly the term "child-centered classroom," an intricate part of educational jargon, could be misunderstood if it were to be

---

* To those unfamiliar with this word (pronounced 'tooke') a toque is a knitted hat that fits the head snugly and can be pulled down over the ears in cold weather.

equated with overindulging children. The goal of the child-centered classroom, however, is to provide an environment where children are able to see themselves as a valued part of a community of learners. In these classrooms, children find personal meaning in new learning experiences, both socially and academically. They set their own pace. Their experiences are welcomed so that they might use them to make the curriculum meaningful. It is a community that survives because of the originality each person breathes into it and that respects the time each needs to develop self-knowledge and self-reliance.

MEETING EDUCATIONAL AND SOCIAL NEEDS

To encourage the unique self of each child, we must give our children the chance to hypothesize, think, make decisions, feel frustration, experience challenge (according to *their* conceptions, not those of adults), solve problems, daydream, tell stories, and make mistakes. I was traveling to the city one chilly, winter afternoon with a friend and her five-year-old daughter, Sebrena. Sebrena, who was tucked safely in her car seat, was telling a story about her day. When she finished, I asked her if she had another story. She smiled as she pulled off her blue toque and said "I have another story in my toque." The story is the way we, at any age, come to know.

For children to meet their educational and social needs as they journey into the next millennium, we must make our classrooms child-centered. The environment must be warm and nurturing — a place where children have the opportunity to "story"[1] as they match their experiences with the experiences of others, as well as with the curriculum — so that learning is personal and meaningful. The foundation for healthy self-esteem is laid when children continue to trust themselves as learners. In the child-centered classroom the curriculum is no longer front and center; it *supports* learning. Learning cannot only be a textbook, a compilation of facts, or a one right way to solve a problem.

---

[1] I use the term "story" to mean talking from personal experience and reflecting to make learning meaningful.

LINKING EXPERIENCES AND PASSIONS WITH LEARNING

As children link their experiences and passions with the learning task, the child-centered classroom encourages them to make decisions that help them become self-teachers. Curriculums are merely guides to enable children to meet the next challenge; children will show us when they need the strategies and skills that are outlined in them. The learning begins with the children as they story. I have discovered that as I internalize the curriculum I am able to let the children show me the way. They, unaware of the opportunity they give me to identify with them as learners, continue to provide gentle nudges that remind me not to hurry the precious, academic process of their becoming self-teachers.

As the grade-one class is involved in writing, they ask how to make the letter that has the "t" sound or the "p" sound or "what makes *ing*." As the teacher, I have to tuck away the feeling that I should stop this self-motivated learning and teach the children all of the letters of the alphabet and the accompanying sounds. I have to remind myself that the need for such lessons in isolation will have little to do with the stories that are being written from real, live, meaningful experiences. Teaching the transition from speech to print is an important part of the curriculum for first grade; however, in a child-centered classroom each child makes decisions about what he needs to get the job done. As the children show the way I become aware of when and how to help them use the curriculum to support their learning. Knowledge of the student's actual level and the level he can achieve with guidance is evident in this nurturing environment.

In the traditional classroom the students are involved in reading to answer teacher-led questions, and writing is often seen by the student as something to edit. To come to know reading and writing as supports for learning personally isn't readily discovered by the students. There isn't time.

As a teacher, I need to know the skills that the children will require during whole-class mini-lessons. An example of a mini-lesson presented itself one morning when one of the students handed a copy of his published story to each of his peers. The story, which turned into an action song about bears (the theme at the time), included many *ing* words — climbing, rolling, eating, fishing, sunning, walking, hibernating, snoring. The song was charted and sung. This became a meaningful way to introduce the "ing" ending, a part of the curriculum. The curriculum supported by theory is, and must be, a vital part of a child-centered classroom.

Children make their learning happen from moment to moment. The following insight could have been easily overlooked, as I collected the children's math, if I hadn't heard Sergei quietly voice his fascination with one of the problems. The purpose of the problems was a quick evaluation of a concept. The recess bell had rung and Sergei hadn't looked at the other three problems due to the unique twists that he was adding to the first problem, resulting in some in-depth subtraction — he had transferred the word problem about the ten bears fishing into a picture problem. (See figure 2.1.)

I joined him to see what his plans were for finishing his math. He explained he knew that "ten bears went fishing," and he added with a grin, "with fishing rods." He continued, "If two bears went away, probably because they were bored, there would be eight left, but this one is mad and ten take away one would be nine. These four are upside down." He chuckled, "And nine take away four would be five. This one is whistling." As he spoke he quickly transferred the picture story into mathematical equations.

Sergei was creating a challenge for himself with the problem because, if I read between the lines correctly, he, not the two bears, was bored. Sergei enjoyed his recess and actually finished the other problems when I handed the papers back a day later.

It becomes continually evident not to control the direction of learning if I am to be included from the best seat in the house. My role, as teacher, changes from that of a dispenser of knowledge to that of a facilitator and guide. The challenge is to know when to be an observer, when to model, and when to stand back to give

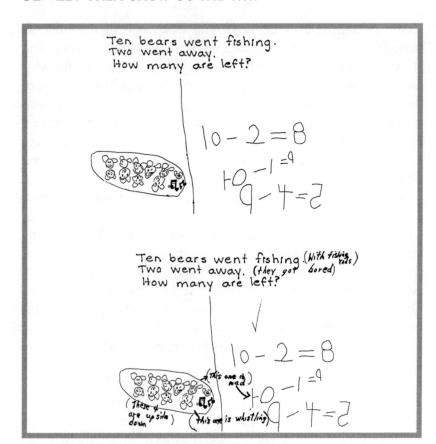

Figure 2.1: Sergei, a grade-one student, has transferred a math problem into a picture problem. The notes in parentheses were written by the teacher to save Sergei's oral talk.

children time to understand. I sense that I have only touched the tip of the iceberg concerning the art of teaching. I am still learning to give myself time to understand where children are coming from and to see that opportune moment to guide them in their personal discovery of how to bridge experiences with new learning. It is a personal process, where frustration, experimentation, daydreaming, and decision making are the very fiber of a child-centered classroom and one that enables children to come to know their unique self, within the larger picture of becoming an independent learner. Could it be said, then, that the child-centered classroom is the environment where a child is able to naturally outgrow self-centeredness while continuing to nurture a positive self-concept and a love for learning?

* * *

In the following scenarios, students are making decisions about their learning. They internalize skills and strategies as they become involved in self-initiated projects and writing to learn. Their support system is good literature, their peers, and a guiding teacher. Their learning environment is a child-centered classroom. The theme, designed to facilitate the learners, is Magic and Make Believe.

LITTLE BOY BLUE RIDING HOOD

Wesley, a serious child, set himself apart in the classroom. He didn't quite see himself fitting in with his peers. He was continually bound up in thought as he sat with a picture of his dad on his desk. We suggested, encouraged, and modeled but everything he did he left half-heartedly in the beginning stages.

Shortly after the reading of several versions of *Little Red Riding Hood*, which was prompted by a serious debate among everyone in the class about the fact that their Little Red story was different, Wesley began to change.

I soon noticed he didn't require the usual help and reassurance. He began to read voraciously. His writing and drawings were flowing independently onto the page. He trusted himself as he used both temporary and conventional spelling to save his rush of thoughts. He had begun to make sense of his world both at home and at school when he wrote *Little Boy Blue Riding Hood.*

His story is about a young boy who encounters a coyote in the elevator while taking a basket of food to his father who lives in an apartment in a faraway city. Changes in Wesley's own home life were being understood as he was able to bridge his world of reality, imagination, and dreams with the world of story.

This is a classic example of how books may play a vital role by helping a child understand that he can be in control and capable of making learning decisions for himself. Wesley's journey through fantasy, as he pored over various versions of *Little Red Riding Hood*, helped him deal with his reality. He grew, personally and socially, as a result of his interaction with literature in a nurturing, child-centered environment.

PRINCE ALLIGATOR

Jade was always the first one to drop an independent project and sit ever so close as stories were being read throughout the school day. It seemed she literally lived in the story, drinking in every detail. One day, as we explored the works of Hans Christian Andersen, something was missing. It was the silent, but intense, intellectual presence of Jade. (You can always feel these students with such a thirst for "knowing" beside you.) She had a story to tell and was off to write.

Skillfully, she was weaving a new story using established patterns found in fantasy literature. It had been a delightful and natural process for Jade as she internalized a sense of story schema (such as "once upon a time" and the theme Good Over Evil) from her author friends and mentors.

Prince Alligator (see figure 2.2) is one of the many stories that were to follow her newly discovered talents. Jade had begun to model the language and story structure of quality books. The credit belongs to these young learners as they take their learning in novel directions. I sense that no amount of long hours, planning contrived lessons at my kitchen table the evening before class, would result in Jade's self-drive to move from speech to print, as she synthesizes her newly discovered knowledge.

The natural process included listening and reading every fairytale she could find. She wrote her own fairytales, which she turned into plays, and she created puppet plays, dioramas, and flannel boards to share with her community of learners. She drew maps and detailed storyboards for her own stories as well as for her favorite classics such as *Rumpelstiltskin*. All of these tech-

Prince Alagater

1. once upon a time in the heart
of spook wood there was a casle
the sight was buteful flowers
were blaming and there tall green
pine trees every where but who
lived in that casle was not buteful
an ugly old witch lived in it about
every day someone went by that
buteful casle and every one who
did was turned into an Alagater by the
witch and thorn into the mote
and it just hoped one day that a
prince came riding along by that
casle (poof!) he was turned
into an Alagater and into the mote
he went leeving muddy foot prints
behind him

2. hanhaa! said the witch got you
the Alagater just snorted.
the neyst day a prinsses came
riding along on her roval hose
sne saw the buteful flowers
she bent Down and picked some
suddnly the wtch came out hee hee
hee sne siad the little prinsses
turned and faced the witch you
my fine prinsses can be my
slave and she locked her up
in the dungon help

she cride suddnly the Alagter
who was a prince stuck his
head up this made the prinsses

3. more scared ohh she cride
but the Alagter siad do not be
scard I'm relly a prince
the witch turned me into an
Nagater oh you por thing
she blew a kiss to him
suddnly he turned into a
hansom prince the princ
called thank you now I'll com
and save you. there was a rope
beside the castle he grabed
it and threw it up to the
window it raped around a bar
and pulled it out then
the rope came dagling down

4 then he threw the rope
up to the princess and
siad climd down
the princess was scared
but she said shed do any
thing to get away from
the witch she climbed
down very slowly the
prince carried her out of
the mote and they
walked throue the woods
and went to the princesses
castle where they where
moried and

5. as for the witch when she
found out that one of her
Alagaters had gon and that the
prinsses had too she disided to
be good so she turned all the
other Alagaters back into peple
and from that day on
every body lived happily
ever after.
THE
N
D

Figure 2.2: Jade demonstrates her understanding of the story structure and language of fairy-tale literature.

niques were modeled by everyone else in the community of learners. She also experimented with many other techniques as she took her learning in many directions.

THE SORCERER'S APPRENTICE

John, a tiny, sparkling red-headed boy, sat each day swallowed up by the smallest desk the custodian could find. He loved to wiggle into that desk, a space he could call his very own in "real school." He came each morning intent on becoming a reader, with his favorite stories from home, and a look that said, "I have more." He had found a way to bridge his home world with the environment at school.

John and his parents were reading a story each evening, a family bedtime ritual, and each morning John arrived to retell another part of the ongoing saga. Confidently, he would fill page after page with pictures and scribble writing, using wonderfully strong, vivid colors. The letter *B* was the first letter that John showed an understanding of in his writing of the story. (See figure 2.3.) It was meaningful to him because of his high interest in the story that he was writing/retelling from home each day at school. (He soon found a need for the rest of the alphabet and the respective sounds.) The oral retelling was published, and John's self-confidence and love for learning grew as he shared his stories with each of his classmates. These published stories were, in turn, taken home by the children and shared with their parents. John's delightful version of *The Sorcerer's Apprentice* was enjoyed by ever-widening audiences.

* * *

"They have to be told." Can a teacher entrusted with the privilege of guiding the learning of children really think this? Children, even young children, want to stand on their own two feet. The questions they have provide them with opportunities to shed the bonds of self-centeredness and become increasingly focused.

"Once upon a time there was a mouse
named Mickey and he lived with a
Wizard. Mickey had to do all the work
and the wizard never had to do anywork.
But one day the wizard went away and he
left his magic hat on the table.
Mickey put the magic hat on...."

"He tried to put a spell on a broom
and he said work broom, work ...
The broom broke to pieces but the
pieces were starting to do something.
More and more brooms were getting made...."

Figure 2.3: Excerpts from John's story. The oral retellings (on the right) were written by the teacher to save John's oral talk.

Wesley made sense of his changing home world, Jade discovered about using writing to learn, and John naturally became a reader as he came to school each day with his story. These children, enjoying the child-centered classroom, were inspired to devote time and energy as they made decisions about their learning.

* * *

Join me as I lean over the fence to speak with Ace, a mature, serious, little blond boy with big brown eyes. He was busy in his driveway beside his city home, collecting rocks. We smiled at each other and I couldn't resist asking him if he was starting first grade in September. "I don't really want to go to school," he said, lining his rocks up on a long flat board. "But I want to go to find out where rocks come from. I'm not sure if they grow or if they...." He attentively placed a tiny rock by a larger one. "I'm pretty sure they grow. They must, 'cause where else can they come from?"

Ace is already forming his own hypothesis. The responsibility of the educator will be to foster that thinking to bring about learning without Ace having to be told.

Ace will enter his classroom on that first day with his pockets bulging and a great story of his own invention about the origin of his rocks. (A community of learners wouldn't be complete without a rockhound. It is a given that rock collections must have a place of honor in the classroom and the book area has *The Beginning Knowledge Book of Rocks and Gems*.[2]) His passions and interests, supported by the stories from the toques of his peers, will support and enrich learning in a child-centered classroom. Meaningful education is profoundly personal!

---

[2] This book has a wonderful section entitled "Rocks in Your Backyard." The author, Jay Heavilin (1964) asks the question, "Where do backyard rocks and pebbles come from?" He shares some thought-provoking theories. This could lead to *The True Book of Rocks and Minerals* (1958) in which Illa Podendorf includes a section, "Some Rocks Are Made From Other Rocks." Peter Parnall creates an awareness of nature's beauty and endurance that "the Rock is much more than a huge lump on the forest floor..." in his book, *The Rock* (1991). Ace, as he experiments with writing and illustrating his own stories, will enjoy how Dick Gackenbach (1981) weaves fact with fiction in *McGoogan Moves the Mighty Rock*, his endearing journey story about the friendship between a boy and a rock.

3

THE TEACHER
AS FACILITATOR:
Getting Started

Learning is finding out what you already know. Doing is demonstrating that you know it. Teaching is reminding others that they know just as well as you. You are all learners, doers, teachers.

– Richard Bach, *Illusions*

A community of learners is a natural collaborative approach that encourages life-long learning. It is an innovative teaching approach that is the key to putting into practice the exciting challenges that are the core of the paradigm shift in education. The much-talked-about shift is not an add-on nor is it another swing of the pendulum. Rather, it is a philosophy with labels such as program continuity, whole language, differentiation, child-centered classroom, inclusive classroom, teachers as facilitators, and parents as partners. It verifies for teachers that now is the time to understand these labels as the core, the part of a whole that supports and encourages them to look through new eyes and to listen with new understanding as children struggle to find their voices. We must welcome these voices as we use the questioning approach to help students learn to question as they grow to accept the responsibility of meeting their learning needs.

THE QUESTIONING APPROACH

When responding to children's questions, it is usual to go into long explanations or ask other questions, then prompt the child to help clarify an issue. The difference behind the questioning approach is to listen, ask a question, and "move on," always indirectly conveying the message to the student that he can solve the problem with *his* ideas. This concurs with the words of John Holt (1983, 12):

> We think in terms of getting a skill first, and then finding useful and interesting things to do with it. The sensible way, the best way, is to start with something worth doing, and then, moved by a strong desire to do it, get whatever skills are needed.

In a community of learners, literacy emerges in rich, natural ways. The questioning approach is to facilitate learning as children are motivated to reach for "whatever skills are needed." As they see themselves as a part of a context that is meaningful, they begin to take responsibility for meeting their own needs.

Aspen

Meet Aspen, a quiet, little native girl who sat at the edge of the kindergarten class. Each day her teacher asked about her story. Aspen's picture was black (see figure 3.1a). She whispered, "I am playing with Tim," as the teacher took her dictation (see figure 3.1b).

One day I joined Aspen's class to demonstrate a community of learners. I asked the children to gather around their table in a circle to write. I talked about dreams as a possible theme. A few of the children began to draw, scribble, and scatter a few letters around their illustrations to save their stories. Some were talking among themselves. They naturally seemed to know "that the words which become the starting point for learning to read and

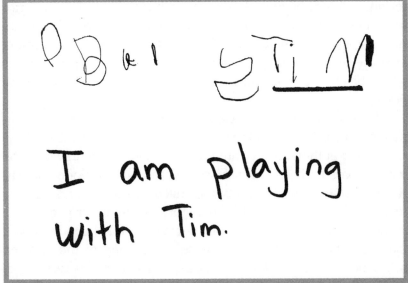

Figure 3.1: (a) Five-year-old Aspen draws a picture using black scribbles; (b) Aspen's dictated copy.

write come from the kids' ideas and not from the teacher's reading book" (McConaghy 1985, 19).

Some of the students joined by watching others; however, Aspen shyly remained at the edge. I had been sitting in the circle drawing and writing with the community. I sometimes read from my writing but when a hush came over the group it seemed an opportune time to read from good literature. (I find that children identify with the characters and happenings in stories, which, in turn, seems to instill them with confidence.) I wanted to help Aspen find her context in the community. I began reading: "Close your eyes and you can be sound asleep in an apple tree or if you like a ship at sea...or with a friend in a robin's nest" (Marzollo 1978).

Aspen moved closer, watching, listening first to the story, then to her classmates as they shared their stories and illustrations. (I find illustrations rise from a young author's page to assist with the telling. I cannot overemphasize the importance of drawing prior to writing: illustrations, twinned with oral telling, are the beginning steps to shaping a story line. Children come to know themselves as authors, building the foundation for reading that occurs when the child joins an author as he predicts, forecasts, and questions.)

The students began to ask questions and offer comments as they naturally built onto their own learning as well as that of the presenting author. At the same time, Aspen began drawing, and we observed that she was scattering a few letters. Soon she was ready to share. Her black eyes sparkled as she held up her picture, and before she could tell her story, a few of her peers commented on the bright colors. She smiled and told her story about playing outside on the green grass. When one of the children asked her if she was lonely, she explained that she wasn't because she had an imaginary friend. Aspen saw herself in a context that was meaningful for her. (See figure 3.2.)

I noticed her teacher and her native liaison, who had been observing, exchange smiles. Initially, Aspen's teacher and I had some concern about taking a child's dictation. When did it pro-

Figure 3.2: Aspen sees herself in a context that is meaningful for her. Note her imaginary friend is represented only by hair.

vide scaffolding? When did it hinder independence? But, we also discussed the magic that occurs when children take charge of their own learning within the nurturing setting of a community of learners.

SETTING UP THE CLASSROOM

The physical appearance of the classroom is one in which the desks, arranged in a circle, are a home base for the community of learners. They write, talk, listen, and bring their own experiences as they link learning across the curriculum. Students use the empty space in the center of the circle to make sense of ideas and concepts though mime, reader's theater, role plays, dance, or reciprocal teaching (chalk talk — drawing and diagramming at the chalkboard — by the student to further explain his premise).

TEACHER POSITIONS

In this community of learners, the teacher, as a guide and facilitator, has three basic positions. These are:

1. Position A: to instruct

2. Position B: to participate, to encourage, and to model for students as they individualize their learning

3. Position C: to observe and evaluate the novel ways children make their learning personal; to prepare for differentiating lessons when assisting one child, a group of children, or the whole class as "they reach for that needed skill" (Holt 1983).

Position A. The teacher sits or stands in the center of the circle to ask the whole community to focus on listening to good litera-ture, a lesson, or directions. During the focus time the teacher may move to the chalkboard or other areas, but the expectation is that this is a teacher-directed time (see figure 3.3a).

Position B. The teacher sits within or close to the circumference of the circle to join the community to write, to share, to listen to children reading, or for a mini-lesson[1] with one student or with a small group of students. Students may come to the teacher or the teacher may, sitting on a low stool, move around the inside of the circle to work face-to-face with one or more students. (This avoids hovering over a student from behind or from the side.) Differentiation is accommodated as this becomes a time to move from student to student encouraging beginning readers to image

---

[1] A mini-lesson becomes a personal time to listen to a child explain how he sees a concept. This is followed by a question to help the student see things in a new light and understand the concept in greater depth. The teacher observes, questions, and sometimes presents a direct lesson.

Figure 3.3a: In Position A, the teacher stands in the center of the circle and the students focus on her.

the story line, to circle known words, to join a peer to read and discuss, or to read independently. This is when a teacher balances her role as participant/observer to encourage independence. A teacher is able to alter her teaching style to accommodate a child's learning style and place along the continuum of the curriculum (see figure 3.3b).

Position C. The teacher is outside the circle, observing the members of the community interacting with one another. This becomes a time when students' questions and comments concerning their math problems, scientific discoveries, writing, and reading of both fiction and nonfiction, are discussed and solved collaboratively (see figure 3.3c).

The teacher slips in and out of the three positions (A, B, and C) as she facilitates and guides a community of learners to facilitate and guide their own learning. Teachers who have observed

Figure 3.3b: In Position B, the teacher moves about the circumference of the circle and works one-on-one with the students.

Figure 3.3c: In Position C, the teacher observes from outside the circle as the students interact with one another.

my community of learners in action say they do many of the things I do but find it difficult to "wait" — that is, give students time to come up with ideas, possibilities, and solutions — as I do. They feel they need to jump in and instruct, suggest, or redirect because they're afraid the lesson might get out of hand or not go according to preconceived plans. I, on the other hand, slip around the outside of the circle and nip little problems in the bud so that the community is able to continue probing, discussing, thinking, diverging, and experiencing the bumpy road of conversation before reaching consensus. As a community they arrive at conclusions, definitions, or answers that everyone is comfortable with or, at least, prepared to live with. Often the consensus is more questions. When I am in Position C, I have to be careful about the student who is squiggly, but about to guide the thinking into an entirely new and much needed direction. The evolution of original ideas is fragile and requires a nurturing environment.

Time spent in Position C is time to observe. I find that as my students come to trust themselves as learners and to know that their voices are welcome, I am able to slip into Position C for longer periods. It is a time when I shape ideas for meaningful lessons for one student, a few, or the whole class. My observational skills are heightened by a clear understanding of the curriculum, and by my belief that learning is a process.

The outer edge of the classroom provides space for many things: a thematic collection of good literature, articles, songs, and poetry; task cards encouraging higher-level thinking; pictures, puzzles, mazes, and brain teasers; manipulatives; a mini class library; a music center; a painting center; bulletin boards; supplies; and visitors.

The centers, which can be changed, added to, or combined, are supports ready to facilitate students as they make decisions while constructing their learning. The built-in message is that the art of communication is valued as the community of learners build onto their ideas as well as onto the ideas of others. The materials are there to support the learning, not to prescribe it.

Students become involved in learning as a process rather than as lessons with a predetermined outcome.

Those who equate learning with children all sitting in a row, their hands on their laps quietly listening, and twenty-five identical pieces of art work or written paragraphs all displayed neatly on the wall, usually leave my classroom thinking, "No learning is going on in that room!" Visitors have to stay for a good block of time to get a perspective of what is really happening. Initially, many question the informal environment in which I view mistakes as learning and I give the students time to implement self-control as long as they are not interrupting the learning of others. One teacher, who sat in my classroom for a week, remarked that it took her awhile to stop looking for teacher-directed lessons. Today, she is a kid watcher. Dr. Vladimir Chubarikov,[2] vice dean of mathematics at Moscow State University, was impressed with the way children working in a community of learners blend creativity and logic. "Their thoughts and ideas are very logical for six year olds," he remarked. "I believe this is because of the teaching they receive in this conducive environment."

A supportive environment is the catalyst that frees children to blend "creativity with logic" as they communicate to internalize their learning.

THE HIDDEN STRUCTURE

In my classroom, the structure is hidden — the children see themselves as having choice, yet as they become involved they live the guiding parameters every moment of the day. These include

◆ respecting one another's learning space

◆ not being judgmental

◆ building onto ideas

---

[2] Dr. Chubarikov's visit was arranged and hosted by the University of Calgary, Centre for Gifted Education.

◆ avoiding stepping on anyone's words

◆ focusing during a requested lesson to link a concept, skill, or strategy that could be the next rung of a child's personal learning ladder

The implications are far-reaching as the community of learners may include visiting children from other age groups, teachers, administrators, parents, and visitors from all walks of life. The mentorship from these incoming members enriches the learning. However, they, too, must internalize the role of a facilitator, stepping back to sense the special rhythm that is at the nucleus of each community of learners — a rhythm that supports the uniqueness of each child in his quest to learn.

The implication of the hidden structure for teachers is to internalize the role of facilitator, as the community of learners creates a learning energy that will leave adults in awe. This approach becomes meaningful when reflective writing and professional collaboration take the place of lessons that become, in essence, the teacher's project — marking papers late into the night, trying to write responses to children's personal writing, or cutting and pasting lessons together for the next day. When you plan rather than prepare every detail, you take away student choice. Lessons prepared from the curriculum, in which the students demonstrate their understanding of the objectives, rather than planned activities, become ongoing projects for the learner.

I recall Janelle, a first grader with curly red hair, dutifully completing a worksheet that instructed her and her classmates to draw a truck, color it green, then draw two sheep in the box of the truck. She drew one large sheep, then turned to a friend, "I drew two sheep in the back of my truck. Can you find them?" It wasn't long before most of the students were adding their ideas as to the whereabouts of the second sheep. "Is it in the front seat? Is it under the truck? Is it under the hood? Is it invisible?"

Janelle, with a little giggle, asked, "Do you give up?" When it appeared that there were no more suggestions she said, "The sheep in the back of my truck is pregnant. See, its big tummy is hanging down." Children interacting in a community of learners are able to bring life even to a worksheet, something that would not be possible were they given the worksheets to take home and mark up.

To be a facilitator means to listen with the community to find those teachable moments to help students discover skills and strategies. Janelle opened a door for a teachable moment. I charted the children's questions, taking advantage of the opportunity to model the use of question marks and have children experience high-frequency, low-interest words — such as *but, if, the, why, when,* and *where* — in a meaningful context.

The teacher who joins a community of learners models an insatiable appetite for learning as naturally as she breathes. For parents the implication is to become a partner in their child's learning. This means reading about children and how they learn, internalizing the art of questioning, and using and understanding writing as a tool for learning. Parents become a part of this approach by attending workshops, where they share ideas and enjoy education as a process. They come to realize that this process is lived and ongoing.

THE FIRST DAY OF SCHOOL

On the first day of school the children arrive in my classroom to find desks arranged in a semi-circle. They choose a desk to be their home base. I give them a piece of Manila tag with their name printed in large letters on it and ask them to write and draw around their name about their world (for example, favorite toys, books, games, things they like to do). They share these with their new-found community of learners. The name strips are eventually secured to the front of each child's home base (desk).

The parents who wish to stay are encouraged to melt in without rescuing their child. When the children feel they are finished personalizing their name card, I find an opportune time to personally give each child a scribbler in which he will make decisions about his learning as he writes to learn. It isn't long before the children who have not yet received their scribblers are reminding me that I haven't given them their book. (This is a first deliberate step in handing over ownership for their education. It is from such little things — for example, seeing me "forget" who I gave scribblers to — that they begin to take the initiative. I feel I'm on the right path when children begin to reach on that first day.) A scribbler is truly a place where students can continue to trust themselves as learners even though they are in school. Throughout the year, they clutch the scribbler like a blanket or an old teddy bear. They decorate it, draw, scribble write, scatter letters, and are encouraged to share their discoveries with classmates. (Actually, by the end of the year each child has filled many scribblers, which are numbered and stacked on a shelf for reference.) Through scribblers, I am able to observe, from the edge, how each student uses his personal world to make his learning meaningful. I also give a scribbler to the parents so that they experience becoming part of the community. Soon everyone is coloring, writing, and chatting. They, to repeat Holt's words, start "with something worth doing, and then, moved by a strong desire to do it, get whatever skills are needed."

On that first day we also take time out to investigate the outer edges of the classroom. We visit all of the centers, discussing how we can use them to build onto learning — the mini-library, painting, music, and materials from the theme center are ways to share a message or to expand on ideas that often take shape during the writing and sharing within the community of learners. As the year goes on, the students become experts at using the centers as resources in all subjects.

We may stop to read a good book. Stories are introduced naturally as part of the support for learning. Throughout the year, time to listen to good literature happens sporadically many times during the day: a story for one child during the morning writing to parallel his story; a story for a group to help stretch an idea; or a story for a whole class to model beginnings, endings, journeys. Whatever its purpose, a story is always to enjoy.

Figure 3.4: The student standing on the seat of her desk is ready to share her writing with her classmates.

Day one, then, sets the stage for a community of learners to write, talk, question, read, and listen as the children construct their learning together.

INFORMAL SHARING

When a student is ready to share his writing, the others may listen or continue writing, but all chatting must stop. The student stands on the seat of his desk and reads (see figure 3.4). The writing is not published as it is work-in-progress at this point in time. Following the reading the author asks the audience if there are any questions or comments. Everyone's voice is valued. This is the beginning of thinking of writing as a tool to learn and is encouraged across all of the subject areas (see chapter 6). It is the key to discovering what you already know and to reach for new skills and new understandings of concepts in meaningful contexts. As Donald Graves (1983, 238) says: "The child who can take control of his information will soon take control of mechanical conventions."

If you are wearing your traditional teacher's hat, take it off for a moment and join a community of first graders writing and talking to learn. It is 8:30 a.m. and children are chatting, reading, drawing, singing — but mostly chatting. There are many burning issues and first-ever experiences to be shared since they left school yesterday.

I find this a prime time to join them (partly in Position B, mostly in Position C) to listen, to learn of their new discoveries, their concerns, interests, likes, and dislikes. They are learning to be a community of learners. The atmosphere of the classroom is electric as the students reflect and share experiences.

FORMAL SHARING

When writing is completed, it is published and becomes part of a book. The original work is on one page and the conventionally typed copy is on the opposite page. The conventionally typed copy is run off into a class set for the author to distribute to his classmates and read during reading time.

Reading time is a whole-class activity and everyone is expected to set individual projects or their writing aside and focus their attention on the author's writing. Differentiation occurs as each student reads his copy in whatever way he finds best (for example, circling words he knows; imaging to understand the writing line; mapping the events of the story in order; reading with a peer; reading quickly and finding other supporting stories, articles, poems, or songs from the theme center or the mini-library.) The author must be available for further questions and comments (such as "What kind is your dog?").

It is also a time when I move about the inside of the circle (Position B) listening to children read as they invite me when they are ready. Parents also join to listen and guide. Children are encouraged to partner-read thus freeing the teacher to spend more one-on-one time with children who are at that special teachable moment. At the beginning of the year there are many who are finding their wings through illustrating with lots of wonderful color. I find time to read the published story with them, using expression that encourages the sense of wonder and that models the flow of language. This special time ends as the community of learners is asked to focus while the author of the morning (the published author) stands on his desk to formally read his writing and entertain any further questions or comments. I find this an opportune time to move about the outside of the circle (Position C) to view the imaging.[4] It is a given that everyone must image to encourage deeper comprehension and further questioning.

I then find a time (Position A) at the close of the discussion to draw everyone's attention to basic skills such as how to sound and write the letter of the alphabet that "dog" begins with, how to build a family of words from the word "dog" by changing the initial letter, how many times "and" is in the writing. I encourage reciprocal teaching as the children take the chalk and work quickly to image the events in the writing. I encourage the class to turn over their copy of the writing and practice the letter that "dog" begins with, and build a word family from the word "dog." If the story is like a poem, I encourage the children to read it using their favorite expression. (This becomes like the old round-robin reading in disguise; however, here the children make the decision to read when they feel comfortable or ask a friend to read with them.) It might also become like reader's theater, using low stools available in the center of the circle. Children who choose to watch are learning in their own way, often following along and memorizing the story (an important prereading skill) before taking it home to share with their parents — I encourage everyone to have the writing in their backpack before leaving for home. I sing, whisper, or say, "Please remind your mother (father, grandfather) to sit down for a cup of coffee while you read and tell her (him) all about the story, the imaging, and the special word fun on the back of the page."

---

[4] I use imaging to mean sketching or using symbols to show an understanding of what is being read. This strategy is especially helpful for students with artistic strengths.

Figure 3.5: Two students are miming to understand the story line.

Invariably I am reminded, "My mother doesn't drink coffee." So I say, "tea, water, wine?" If I see them still shaking their heads then I say, "Ask them to listen to see if they have any questions or comments about the writing, or teach your teddy bear. He will be an excellent audience." We, as teachers and parents, must sow the seeds for learning to be continuous, natural, and personal. As the children settle in, they will begin to trust themselves as learners, and stop asking "Is this okay, teacher?" or saying "I can't."

BARRY AND AMANDA

Barry, a typical, energetic grade-one student, flew by, still in his coat and cap, remarking something about another chapter for his bike story. Conrad, curious as usual, looked up smiling and asked, "Can you ride your bike without falling over?" Barry stopped and the two boys became deeply engrossed in conversation. Barry demonstrated, using mime to knit his concrete experience with oral expression before writing. This happened in the center of the circle of desks (see figure 3.5).

I constantly observe children laughing, frowning, and questioning as they show genuine interest and understanding for their classmates' feelings, ideas, and discoveries. I recall Merron Chorny (1988, 2) saying: "Expressive language is simultaneously both the context and the instrument for exploration and discovery." At the risk of being redundant this is a time for me to gain insight for guiding learning more effectively, to determine the focus for whole-class lessons, to sense the right timing for an individual mini-lesson, to share a word of encouragement and, most important, to avoid rescuing a child on the brink of discovering a concept for the first time.

The challenge for me is to know when to change my role from that of an observer (Position C) to that of a participant (Position B). The storytelling appears to be the budding stage when children develop a sense of story as they integrate their world with the various disciplines of the school world. I need to understand the writing process to avoid curtailing the oral flow of storytelling as children move from speech to print. They must be free to naturally experiment with the semantics, syntax, and graphophonemics of the language as they talk and write.

The transition period from speech to print is not only filled with squiggles on a page but is also a time when students are unable to remain focused, make decisions, and are reluctant to trust their ability. The parents and I talk about when to observe and when to participate. It is also time when we, as adults, must be supportive without rescuing. It is important to remember that, given the opportunity, children take ownership for learning in their classroom as naturally as they do outside of the classroom.

I couldn't have possibly preplanned the mini-lesson that assisted Amanda's self-discovery. Amanda was standing beside me clutching five pages of her story from the previous day, in which she had been totally engrossed. She was upset as she explained that she couldn't find her words. Until this point Amanda had captivated her audiences with her "telling" stories, as she called them. Her only reference would be a sketchy illustration symbolically representing her oral stories. These five pages, packed with strings of letters from her favorite purple crayon, were one of Amanda's first attempts at converting speech to print. It was evident that the initial and final consonants were in place. The timing seemed ripe for modeling a strategy that would help Amanda find her words. I inquired if I could be her secretary and write her story as she told it. As she watched me write, leaving exaggerated spaces between the words, Amanda suddenly relaxed and announced, as she took the pencil from my hand, "I'm going to write my story again." Amanda has never looked back. She had discovered that her long, interesting stories could be saved on the page and retrieved the next day just as she had left them. The timing was right for modeling word boundaries using the strategy of dictation. Happily, Amanda hadn't become too frustrated. For me, it is a thrill to assist that crucial stage of the writing process that enables a child to internalize learning. (See figure 3.6.)

Meanwhile, Barry had moved to the rocket to write the next chapter of his bike story. (In our classroom, the rocket is one of many popular centers. It is a place where a student may have privacy yet be a part of the classroom community. See figure 3.7.)

Soon, the children assembled for sharing; some continued to draw or write while others stopped to listen. Barry wanted to share. He could hardly contain his excitement as he stood on his chair. A hush fell over the busy learners as he began to read.

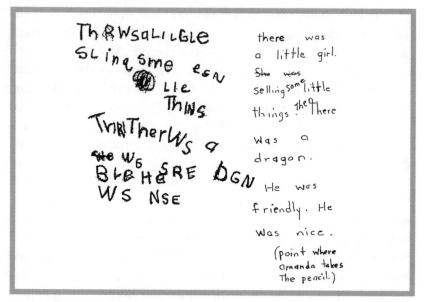

Figure 3.6: On the left is the first page of Amanda's story. On the right, the teacher has written down the words as Amanda dictated.

Figure 3.7: A student spends some quiet time in the rocket.

"I am riding my bike. I was going. Suddenly I hit a rock." (See figure 3.8.)

Barry looked up, smiled, and asked, "Are there any questions or comments?"

"Why did you hit a rock?" Justin asked.

"Well, I wasn't looking because my favorite horse was running in the pasture by the road. He was curious about me riding my bike, and I was busy watching him."

Becky, whose passion is horses, stopped her writing and asked, "Could you write about the horse?"

"Well, I could."

Amanda asked, "Was the rock smooth?"

"No, it was a rough rock," Barry replied with a look of importance. "If it was smooth my bike tire would have glided right over it."

A few minutes passed. It appeared no further comments were forthcoming. I took advantage of the opportunity for a whole-class lesson (Position A) about describing words. At this point we brainstormed a long list of words that would help the students picture the rock that caused the problem (for example, sharp, jagged, pointy, grayish, whitish, blackish, pinkish, and brownish). One intriguing attribute of rocks is color and color was our present theme. Interestingly, a number of students talked about the rhyming pattern "ish." Also, everyone welcomed the information about conglomerate rocks from the class rockhound. Then, there was a short spurt of renewed interest as the class asked Barry, "What happened when you hit the rock?"

Within the community of learners the children share experiences and stories as they ask questions of one another. The author appears to naturally risk as he shares and develops a sense of self. His peers see the pattern, and accept or reject the story. The questioning is sincere, motivated by genuine interest. We, as teachers, have to guard against taking control of our students' conversation, using our teaching skills before the students have discussed all the possibilities, and focusing on mechanics that can stop the flow of students' ideas. Instead, we have to encourage

Figure 3.8: On the left is Barry's bike story. On the right is the published story that Barry handed out to his classmates.

and support their independent learning while they are involved in meaningful conversation. The oral language that accompanies the sharing of the story is richer and more sophisticated than the written at this stage of the process. This is a time for the teacher to slip into Position C.

The community of learners is relaxed, with all members building upon one another's ideas. The presenting author is developing a positive self-concept as he and his peers naturally develop a sense of story. Many students continue their writing and illustrating, stopping periodically to ask the presenting author a question concerning the part they don't understand or commenting on the part of the story they like the best. Questioning in this way is a part of the writing process (Graves 1983).

The visiting parents often join in the conversation with the author and his audience, or share part of a story they are writing. Often parents begin by saying, "I would like to share a story I have written. However, I can't think of a title." Or, in response to the statement, "I can't figure out how to end this story," one mother said, "Stories never end. Authors just have to find a place to jump off."[4]

Another mother was intrigued by her daughter's imaginative storytelling but concerned she was writing her story using continuous squiggles. She asked "Shouldn't I be teaching her the alphabet?" I shared an article by Dorothy Watson entitled, "When Is Language Too Much Too Soon?" Watson's premise is that children will build onto their prior knowledge of oral and written language in readiness for the next stage. A smile of understanding broke over the mother's face as she read the article. The timing was right for yet another member of the community of learners, a mom, to discover what she already knew — it is important for her daughter to make choices about her own learning. The mother was further convinced when a student at the end of grade one who had once used scribbles entered our classroom and shared a story she had written. She had experimented with many stages of the writing process when she was in grade one and was now beginning to incorporate conventional spelling and the mechanics of writing (periods, capitals, and so on). She was further convinced when she observed the grade-one students asking for several readings so that they could mime the action parts. (See figure 3.9.)

At the conclusion of the story everyone gathered on the floor in the center of the circle of desks. It was an opportune time for me (Position A) to model good literature with a story entitled *A Rainbow of My Own* by Don Freeman from a book that was part of the collection of materials in the theme center about Colors and Change. Everyone was focused, so we sang a few songs, written on large chart paper, about colors and rainbows.

This time together after writing, sharing, and reading is usually time to do phonics, spelling, and printing. Everyone is given a blank sheet of paper and I dictate the sounds and names of letters or commonly used words from their stories, such as *the, a, and,*

---

[4] That wonderful idea was shared by a mother who had just returned from a conference about the learning that accompanies storytelling. The guest speaker, Bill Pasernak, made the statement initially.

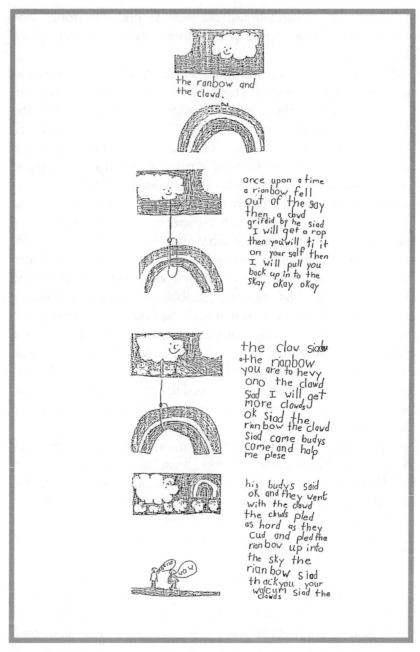

Figure 3.9: This story was written by a student at the end of grade one who has moved naturally from speech to print.

but. Then I write each letter or word on the chalkboard or chart paper, pointing out letter forms and the sounds. This is followed by self-correction and much discussion. This is the time when skills and strategies for forming letters, sounding words, and so on can be shared with the children. Some will be ready to transfer the lessons to their writing the next day. To begin with some will just copy. The whole process is a follow-up to morning language time. It is nonthreatening and a time to transfer oral speech to print. The teacher can build her knowledge bank of strategies and skills necessary for each grade level by reading Mary Tarasoff's wonderful book entitled *A Guide to Children's Spelling Development for Parents and Teachers*. The spelling, printing, phonics times grow through the months and it is exciting to observe (Position C) children naturally transfer their learning, and know what questions to ask, as they make the alphabet work for them when they have a story to save in their scribblers. They continue to understand themselves as learners as they are "moved by a strong desire to do it, get whatever skills are needed."

4
THEMES: Colors and Change/Hiking with Mother Nature

The kite he made an hour ago
now drifts and glides: a bird on wing
above the trees. Yet down below
it is a child who holds the string.

The craft is cradled on the wind.
A dancing colour in the sun
it draws young thought beyond the earth
to where his dreams have just begun.

We must enable the child to hold the string.

– Jannis Hare, *Sky Puppets*

A theme is one way of facilitating the students' activities as they differentiate learning in the regular classroom. Students, as they have access to the theme, have the opportunity to pace themselves, work at different levels of complexity, and choose how they go about making learning meaningful for themselves.

At the same time, themes provide a common thread for the many individual experiences and interests that the children bring to the classroom. The core curriculum is addressed within the themes, and webbed with the children's interests, natural curiosity, and passions. Themes must be designed to support questioning while motivating critical and creative thinking.

Robert and Marlene McCracken (1995, 224-25) explain:

An educational theme is like a musical theme. In a musical theme the same notes recur in different rhythms, keys, forms, and cadences; the theme holds together a series of otherwise unrelated musical expressions. A fully explored theme has many variations....So it is with the educational theme. The exploration takes place within the classroom as the teacher and children work together.

Themes branch in many directions, which the children follow as they explore, write, draw, talk, read, and sing about their interests. Task cards, based on Bloom's Taxonomy (see figure 4.1), encourage us as teachers to appreciate the many levels of thinking that happen by the minute as children transfer their learning from home to school and from school to home (see chapter 5). Task cards provide information that can stretch students' already divergent thinking (see figure 4.2). Some students rely on task cards to steer their learning while others use the cards to complement and enrich what they are already doing. A task card may be chosen by a student or suggested by the teacher to enrich a project; then the information card may be used to build onto a hypothesis. These information cards, which are teacher-made, can be about any topic for which little information can be found for a certain grade level (see figure 4.3). The teacher may hand a task card or an information card to a student at a "teachable moment" or to independent learners who are searching for information or ways to demonstrate their understanding of an idea, hypothesis, or concept. We see the children's wonderings, ideas, suggestions, and nonstop conversations as crucial steps toward shaping the topic.

It is important that teachers know the role implicit in each of the major cognitive operations in Bloom's Taxonomy so they can facilitate students when they are working at one of the levels. What may appear unrelated is held together by the theme and is celebrated as the learning branches into exciting new and wonderful ideas. This is truly a time to understand how the role of teacher and the role of student interchange.

A theme is designed to convey to students that this is their classroom where they will bring their storying (talking from personal experience and reflecting to make learning meaningful),

BLOOM'S TAXONOMY

Knowledge. Bloom (1956,63) defines knowledge as "the recall of specific and isolated bits of information."

The student's role is basically to respond, absorb, remember, recognize, and practice. The teacher's role is to direct, tell, lead, show, and examine.

Comprehension. Comprehension can take on three forms: translation, interpretation, and extrapolation. According to Bloom (ibid., 89,90), "comprehension is based on what is given rather than on some abstraction brought from the other experiences."

The role of the student is to explain, extend, demonstrate, translate, and interpret. The role of the teacher is to demonstrate, listen, reflect, question, compare, contrast, and examine.

Application. Bloom (ibid., 120) defines this as the ability to use some things correctly, when faced with a "...situation in which no mode of solution is specified."

The role of the student is to solve novel problems, demonstrate use of knowledge and constructs. The role of the teacher is to show, facilitate, observe, and question.

Analysis. Bloom (ibid., 144) says analysis "emphasizes the breakdown of the material into its constituent parts...."

The student's role is to discuss, go into detail, uncover, list, and dissect. The teacher's role is to probe, guide, observe, and act as a resource.

Synthesis. Bloom (ibid., 162) defines synthesis as the "putting together of elements and parts so as to form a whole. This includes communicating ideas, feelings, and experiences to others.

The student's role is to discuss, generalize, relate, compare, contrast, and abstract. The role of the teacher is to reflect, extend, analyze, and evaluate.

Evaluation. According to Bloom (ibid., 185), evaluation involves making judgments about the value of something. The evaluative process may prelude the acquisition of all other cognitive skills.

The student's role is to engage in commitment, judge, dispute. The teacher's role is to accept and harmonize.

Figure 4.1: Bloom's Taxonomy

Figure 4.2: These task cards, one for each of Bloom's cognitive domains, were constructed for the theme Hiking with Mother Nature. Dandelions had become the focus that branched from the main theme. Students may select task cards in any order — they do not move sequentially from knowledge through evaluation. Task cards facilitate learning. The students determine how they are used.

Figure 4.2 (cont'd)

theories, and questions. A theme needs to have a supporting collection of good literature, nonfiction articles, poetry, and songs
readily available for enjoyment, as models for writers, and as
challenges to students who often are not aware that they can
write using storying as a tool to learn. Teachers, too, need this
collection of materials and ideas to support that "unexpected"
leap a child takes — a book that bears out his discovery that
drawing, not just writing, is used to save talk; an article that encourages a young scientist to discover how to weave nonfiction
with fiction. Storying is used in the context of students drawing,
talking, using prewriting or conventional writing as they discover
that storying can be a tool to learn in any subject. It isn't limited to
writing a story with a beginning, middle, and end. Storying must
be encouraged as a way to demonstrate understanding of concepts and big ideas (such as the mysteries of rainbows). Children
joining their community of learners at school will discover that
their storying is welcome and can become an invaluable learning
tool. Egan (1986, 1) explains: "the principles about children's

Figure 4.3: Information cards provide an additional resource for students who have chosen a challenging task card.

learning are at best inadequate, and lead us largely to ignore the most powerful tools for learning that children bring with them to school...children's imagination."

* * *

September-October is the time of year that suggests hibernation and a well-deserved rest for Mother Nature. This is also the time our students gather in school settings, to become an active community of learners. Here, each individual discovers himself as a learner whose storying contributes to the vital and unique chemistry of the classroom. This is the time for teachers, too, as catalysts, to join their community of learners, to inspire each member to discover what Smith (1990) describes as "the relationship of instruction to her thinking." If we, as teachers, believe this, then broad universal themes, which branch into mini-themes as the students delve into areas of interest, are a way to "walk our talk." I have found that universal themes are blended into the learning that is ongoing throughout the year.

Colors and Change for the fall theme, for example, invites questions about the mysteries of nature as students freely use colors and scribbles, and talk in quiet, shy tones as they start to make decisions about their school learning. Hiking with Mother Nature is a great theme to slip in with the spring breezes, because it encourages children to explore their precious but vulnerable environment while building on the concepts and skills they have learned throughout the year. These two themes are universal because they are not limiting or restricting and are readily interwoven from backyards to all areas of the curriculum.

THE CURRICULUM: A SILENT PARTNER

Three times during the school year, I review the curriculum for all subjects. At the beginning of each reporting period, I organize the information into a curriculum letter. It outlines both the major learning goals and the specific learning goals for each subject (see figure 4.4). This letter accompanies the anecdotal report card, which facilitates the student-led interviews throughout the term (see chapter 8).

The major goals for each subject are that (1) the students will demonstrate that learning is a process whereby they discover how language works in their learning as they explore, communicate, and construct meaning in and out of school; (2) students be given opportunities to be actively involved as they explain and defend their ideas about concepts, orally and in writing; (3) students be assisted to acquire the basic knowledge, skills, and positive attitudes they will need to be responsible citizens of society;

The purpose of this letter is to

- report your child's progress in relation to the goals of the curriculum
- to report your child's progress in relation to himself/herself

At our school, everyone is a teacher, and everyone is a learner. The students join a community of learners in a nurturing environment to reflect on experiences and to become actively involved as they develop the skills, attitudes, and knowledge as outlined by the educational program of studies. The following goals and themes were the guides in **language arts** for November, December, January, and February.

Major Goal
Students will demonstrate increasing confidence and competence in their abilities to use language to explore, construct, and communicate meaning.

Specific Learning Goals
Students will learn
- to engage in and enjoy the reading, writing, listening, and speaking behavior
- to read, listen, talk about literature, poetry, and song (challenging them to grow as independent readers and writers)
- to predict what might happen next in a story using personal experiences, text, or visual clues (such as titles or pictures)
- to ask questions that will help them understand when discussing and reading
- to select and write about topics of personal interest—while experimenting with pictures, diagrams, symbols, letters, words, or phrases as a means of representing ideas and experiences
- to know how ideas and information can be organized and presented helps understanding and communication of ideas (e.g., stories have openings, events, and conclusions; the difference between fiction and nonfiction; the fact that titles, tables of content, and headings help readers and writers)
- to become aware of organizing talk and writing around a topic

Figure 4.4: Example of the language arts part of a curriculum letter and anecdotal report. There is a letter for each subject.

- to retell the key details or main ideas from a reading or listening experience, and relate what they know to new information and ideas to help draw conclusions
- to respond to stories and poems by expressing opinions and differing viewpoints on what they have read or heard
- to celebrate the development of their ideas by publishing their writing for familiar audiences, and to revise initial writing drafts by adding to ideas or information
- to develop a persuasive argument and to question or respond to others in collaborative learning settings

Student Report

Michelle, as a developing reader, is experimenting with all aspects of the reading and writing process. She demonstrates a desire to create meaning through print. She enjoys and understands what she reads. She organizes her writing from the top to the bottom of the page. She understands the letter/sound relationship and her store of conventional spelling is growing.

Michelle sets goals for herself each day and works intently to meet them. She takes time to share her excellent stories with the community of learners, to ask questions, and to comment to help others to build onto their stories. This will help her develop good listening skills in a meaningful context.

If you have any questions or concerns, please call me at 555-1234.

Yours truly,

Figure 4.4 (cont'd)

and (4) students be provided with the opportunity to extend their curiosity and learn about their natural world and live healthy, active lives. It is the specific learning goals for each subject (see figure 4.4), however, that steer my teaching. (These goals are determined by each province or state.) As the students lead the way I am assured that the basics, though woven into the learning in a meaningful way, are not left out. I observe students living and using these major and specific goals as they become active members in their community of learners.

WEBBING AN OVERVIEW

My next step is to web a skeletal overview (see figure 4.5). I use the web as I plan the materials for the theme. It continues to grow as the students bring their worlds and interests to the learning. It includes good literature, articles, songs, poetry, art ideas, and focuses for whole-class lessons that I can use when a new spurt of energy seems to be needed. I have to remind myself, whenever I think I should be more teacher-directed, to step back and observe how a new spark from the most unlikely student will encourage the students to analyze, synthesize, and evaluate their premises. (See chapter 1.)

While attending to the curriculum and webbing my overview, questions float about daring me to stretch my thinking. Are there rainbows on the moon? Is the sky really blue? Is there a pot of gold at the end of a rainbow? Which color is happy? As I survey the curriculum of studies I appreciate its open design welcoming teachers to encourage students to see the relationship of their commonplace thinking in the world of school.

Then I gather nonfiction and fiction books, articles, pictures, mazes, jokes, information, poems, music, and charts. This becomes an adventure full of surprises — spurred on by imagination and creativity and later enriched by the students. This is the collection of "stuff" that is displayed in the theme center. (See figure 4.6.) (See bibliography for a list of books and articles that would fit into any teacher's theme center.)

A Guide for Teaching, Writing Curriculum Letters, and Planning Themes

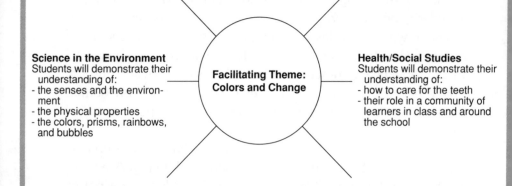

Teacher
The teacher must demonstrate an ability to:
- be aware that reading is a process
- be aware that writing is a process and a tool for learning
- be aware that all children are writers and readers but are at different places along a continuum
- be aware that reading can constitute telling from a picture, either drawn or found in a book, from scribbles or strings of letters followed by temporary spelling of words. Some suggested readings include *Living Between the Lines* by Lucy McCormick Calkins, *A Guide to Children's Spelling Development for Parents and Teachers* by Mary Tarasoff, and *Phonics Phacts* by Ken Goodman.

Language Arts
Students will demonstrate their ability to:
- read independently, illustrate, and talk about their writing.
- read, listen, and talk about good literature, poetry, song, fiction, and nonfiction
- predict what will happen
- question and answer
- listen for enjoyment and for information
- compare stories with a beginning, middle, and end
- use order and time — when, where, before, after, long time, yesterday, today, tomorrow, day of week when storying
- read from left to right
- hear sounds of initial, middle, and ending consonants
- hear rhyming

Science in the Environment
Students will demonstrate their understanding of:
- the senses and the environment
- the physical properties
- the colors, prisms, rainbows, and bubbles

Facilitating Theme: Colors and Change

Health/Social Studies
Students will demonstrate their understanding of:
- how to care for the teeth
- their role in a community of learners in class and around the school

Math
Students will demonstrate their understanding of:
- patterns, similarities, differences, and creating patterns
- transferring a pattern to paper and acting a pattern out with body movements, then talking about the process
- sets, greater than, fewer than, equal to
- shapes, time, counting, numbers, and classification
- creating and completing surveys

Art and Music
Students will demonstrate their ability to:
- use colors as a means of communicating an idea
- use color appropriately when telling a story or using patterns
- use song as a method of telling a story and creating a pattern of sound

Note: These objectives serve only as a guide. As the students show us the way, through their writing, their skills are woven in and around the activities they have selected as a way of meeting the particular objective. Students work from objectives, and the activities then become a vehicle to meet those objectives.

Figure 4.5: Charts like this are used for all subject areas.

Figure 4.6: The theme center facilitates students' writing and projects and often is a resource for students who want to delve deeper into a particular area of interest.

There are as many ways of building a theme as there are teachers; however, the characteristics discussed in this chapter must be visible within the theme. The theme becomes the vehicle that provides the opportunity for students to individualize their own learning, stretch their thinking, and enhance decision making.

Generally, students will select a task of their choice, which usually provides for more opportunity for extended writing or new writing depending on the student.

5

HOW STORIES FOSTER STUDENTS' LEARNING:
Foxes in Literature

Good literature is the tool that enables the community of readers to shift their thinking from "Seeing things the way they are and asking why, to seeing things the way they might be and asking why not."

– Author unknown

M y classroom is a community of learners where the children, the parents, and I join with authors of quality books during the intriguing process of making learning meaningful. As I observe these first graders busily extending their learning in what they term "real school," they rarely question their ability to learn. Learning, after all, has been ongoing for these young children from the moment they took their first breath. They arrived in the "real school," where they continue to learn naturally, experienced at drawing from their environment, their parents, and each other.

I, as learner, teacher, and facilitator, feel privileged to join this community of readers every day. Here, published authors become mentors, as they artfully inspire, influence, broaden, model, support, and provoke.

The following is an example of how children constructed their learning as they became immersed in the literature-based theme, Foxes in Literature.

TYLER

It all started the day Tyler discovered the mounds of fox dens on the southwest quarter of his parents' ranch.

He lived on a ranch where cattle were his center of focus. Then one day he discovered the mounds teeming with red foxes. Tyler proudly shared reports, pictures, and photos he had taken. The excellent map of the fox sightings that accompanies Janet Foster's story *Fox Watch* motivated Tyler to construct detailed maps of the territory frequented by his foxes. Soon, the theme Foxes in Literature, prompted by Tyler's independent study, began to take shape in our classroom.

As they began their journey with books, it wasn't long before the students' visits extended from Tyler's ranch to any part of the world that even hinted at having foxes. Every time that sly, little creature popped out of the pages of another book they were off to discuss, illustrate, and record its location on a large wall map of the world, write stories about trickery, sculpt Brer Fox from a lump of clay, or daydream of running with the foxes. I truly became a facilitator and, in turn, books facilitated my learning as well as the children's.

As Tyler continued to be our inspiration, the focus of the theme gravitated to the world of nonfiction, in which the children could find out information about foxes. Merebeth Switzer's *Red Fox*, with life-like photos and true documentation, was in constant demand. Irina Korschunow's heart-warming journey story, *The Foundling Fox*, was an instant favorite. It wasn't until the academic discussion that followed the reading of the story, *Foxy Fools Fido* that the students began to explore fiction stories. An unknown author had written *Foxy Fools Fido,* a tale about his beloved dog, Fido, who could skillfully fetch things, roll over, and catch a ball. One day Fido was left tethered by a very long leash to a tree, with a tasty dish of liver crumples nearby. As Fido was about to gulp his first mouthful, a fox appeared just beyond the reach of Fido's outstretched leash. Fido began to bark loudly and chase the fox. However, the calculating fox made sure that the chase led Fido in circles around his tree. By the end of the story Fido was wound around the tree, watching helplessly, as the crafty fox ate his crumples.

In the following conversation, note how the children have woven their experiences with the newly discovered ideas from *Foxy Fools Fido* and how they show respect for the opinions of others while confidently adding to their own knowledge.

TEDDY: Fido can do neat tricks, just like my dog. My dog can roll over, too. He can fetch things, even out of water.

PAUL: Those are human tricks, that business of rolling over and fetching. The fox tricks the wild way to get food.

TEDDY: The wild way?

PAUL: Well his tricks are instinctive. No one taught him. The fox knew how to trick.

TEDDY: Fido's tricks didn't help him when he got tricked.

PAUL: Fido's tricks weren't wild tricks.

The entire first-grade class soon joined in. As the rich conversation continued, the children referred to stories in which the fox was tricked, the fox tricked someone else, or there was no trick. We began the journey of reading every fox story we could find. (I might add that there were never enough quality books available.) A group decision was made to put the findings on a large wall chart (see figure 5.1). There were desk-sized charts for anyone who wished an individual chart. The charting during and following the reading of the stories encouraged the children to analyze, synthesize, and evaluate, challenging their higher-level thinking skills (Bloom 1956). As the children became personally involved, the chart proved to be a fun way to discover that stories have themes, plots, and settings. Lively discussions took place daily as the community of learners became intrigued with the sly foxes doing what appeared to be nice things when, in fact, they were just trying to get their own way. Controversial discussions were

Title of Story	Was there a trick?	The fox tricks?	Another animal tricks?	The fox gets tricked?	How does the fox feel in the end?
Fox Eyes	yes	yes	no	yes, maybe	He has forgotten all of the animal's hiding places
Fantastic Mr. Fox	yes	yes	no, men try	almost	happy to have food badger worries
Brer Rabbit and the Wonderful Tar Baby	yes 2 tricks	yes	no, fire	yes	hungry surprised
The Fox and the Crow (fable)	yes	yes	no	no	enjoyed the cheese
Fox Watch (Jane Foster's True Animal Stories)	yes	yes people watching discovered that the vixen changed her habits	no	no	felt safe raising her kits
The Gingerbread Man	yes	yes	no	no	content he loves gingerbread

Figure 5.1: Quality literature provides a natural base from which children can comfortably come to know their personal learning while building on one another's ideas.

stimulated when Badger, in Roald Dahl's *Fantastic Mr. Fox*, asked Mr. Fox if all this stealing worried him. The students then compared Mr. Fox's clever reasoning about no killing being involved to many of their favorite television programs. This, in turn, led to discussions of ways to prevent violence. It also provided an excellent opportunity to develop an awareness for critical viewing.

Ralph Waldo Emerson said: "'Tis the good reader that makes the good book." As the children immersed themselves in fox stories within the community of readers, the ownership for reading was evident. I was kept busy finding ways to accommodate rather than direct the learning. I searched for quality books about foxes to add to the many brought by the children. I became involved in the world of foxes and the threat of their extinction. I was inspired to read and found the opportunity to model as I shared my favorite parts of David MacDonald's *Running With the Fox*. The children had been studying animals in danger of extinction as part of a focus in science. They charted ways to deal with yet another environmental concern.

As the children joined the authors of books about foxes, they created and recreated plays, puppet presentations, poetry, mime, art, and dance. Dance, motivated by George Shannon's *Dance Away*, energized the class to choreograph many original tricky fox trots, hops, and jigs. The popularity of the fables about foxes grew as the children made them come alive through mime.

The children wrote many original stories about foxes and the tricks they were involved in. These were discussed at length before being included with the accomplished authors on the class survey. Marie Hall Ets's book, *In the Forest*, motivated many journey stories. Of course, a sly fox was introduced into the children's stories creating numerous unpredictable problems along the way. As the children read and wrote stories they internalized an awareness of story schema. The maxim, "Give a child a book and watch imagination grow," was clearly demonstrated.

The field trip to observe the foxes on Tyler's farm further helped the class blend life experiences with stories from real authors. Many of the students talked about how much easier it was to picture a setting described in a story after being there. The concept of story and how it can be molded from reality was before our eyes. Truly, these first graders were developing an awareness of how their favorite authors might weave fact with fiction while writing stories, as Irina Korschunow did when she wrote *The Foundling Fox*, a story the children requested countless times.

Making quality books easily available to children enables them to read for enjoyment, validate what they already know, and share what they are thinking. Children's individual needs and learning styles can be met in the regular classroom setting. Learning, even in a nurturing environment with a community of readers in place, would not be as exciting without access to lots of quality books to ensure richness and diversity. Tyler, for example, whose passion area led him to explore and write nonfiction, always found time to join the community of learners, thus gaining as well as adding another point of view. He continued to have us look at the other points of view by sharing his favorite part from Switzer's *Red Fox*: "Sneaky, sly troublemakers — that is how foxes appear in many stories. But real foxes do not deserve this bad reputation. They may seem to be sneaky or sly at times, but they are just being clever in order to hunt for food and escape enemies." Paul joined Tyler as they discovered the parallels between a fiction and a nonfiction story where the "tricks" of the wild are important for survival. On the other hand, Teddy was able to understand his personal learning in context while still having much in common with his peers as he said, "Fido's tricks didn't help him when he got tricked."

Readily available books are the tools that enable a community of readers see things the way they are, as well as the way that they might be. Curiosity is the key that inspires young people to become life-long learners.

6
WRITING FOR SCIENCE:
Questions Not
Answers

When I heard the learn'd astronomer,
When the proofs, the figures, were ranged in columns before me,
When I was shown the charts and diagrams, to add, divide,
    and measure them,
When I sitting heard the astronomer where he lectured with much
    applause in the lecture-room,
How soon unaccountable I became tired and sick,
Till rising and gliding out I wander'd off by myself,
In the mystical moist night-air, and from time to time,
Look'd up in perfect silence at the stars.

– Walt Whitman, *When I Heard the Learn'd Astronomer*

A young Albert Einstein opted out of formal schooling for a time so he could make sense of his developing hypotheses. He was frustrated reading about discoveries on topics that appeared irrelevant to his questions. If he had sat complacently learning about the pure sciences of the previous years, would his theory of relativity have been put on the shelf? Would Newton's theories still be the paradigm that lead the way? Einstein's never ending personal wonderings about time and space led him to make a difference for our world.

How many young scientist sitting in our classrooms today have burning questions that they need to pursue? The spin-off for learning is invaluable.

SCIENCING

In this chapter, join students "sciencing"[1] within the support of their community of learners. As they become involved in their

---

[1] This is a term I use to describe what children do as they bring their worlds of experience to each learning situation.

The young scientist sharing, with a classmate, yet another theory about his mini-greenhouse.

first individual science projects, they are in control of their learning as they naturally use writing, drawing, talking, and listening as tools to help build onto their *own* knowing.

One of many students instrumental in showing me the way was a first grader who literally flew into class each morning with the results of yet another home experiment. Before settling to write and diagram about his big ideas he would talk about them with anyone in his community of learners who gathered to comment and ask questions. They usually had to find their way to his desk through a maze of experiments organized under, around, and on a special table placed in front of his desk.

One interesting investigation, which piqued everyone's interest for over a month, was his mini-greenhouse. It consisted of mounds of dirt in which dandelion seeds, shaped like miniature helicopters, were planted. Each mound was protectively covered with the top of a clear plastic soda pop bottle cut at the neck. With this student, I had the privilege of observing him shape his learning and his learning space, oblivious of the love of learning that he was modeling for his peers. His "mathematical/logical" style of learning, bridged with his ongoing practice of science, complemented his community of learners.

As teachers facilitating learning in our classrooms, we would soon stop spending money on ready-made charts and colorful, expensive equipment, and set our contrived lessons aside, for the opportunity to observe self-motivated students embark on science projects supported by their community of learners. The expression "creativity is messy" would take on new meaning. We would enjoy the world through the questions of children. "Einstein suggested to Piaget that he investigate children's intuitive notions of speed and time, thereby inspiring one of the psychologist's most illuminating lines of research. Einstein stood out among natural scientists in his abiding curiosity about children's minds. He had once declared that we know all the physics that we will ever need to know by the age of three" (Gardner 1993,89).

Students investigate their ideas of science through their own experiences as they work independently, together, or seek help from peers or a facilitating adult in the room. As they talk they improvise. Nachmanovitch (1990,95) writes: "There is a commerce of feeling and information back and forth, exquisitely coordinated. When conversation works, each collaborator brings to the work a different set of strengths and resistances. We provide both irritation and inspiration for each other — the grist for each other's pearl making."

In my classroom, the children were involved in their individual projects, writing, talking, and sharing with their community, which I find encourages self-organization.

To the untrained eye the classroom setting may appear to be in chaos. However, the energy of the community of learners moves toward a self-order as students make new meaning. Thinking is celebrated as children share and grow as learners. Wheatley (1992,150) points out: "In our past explorations, the tradition was to discover something and then formulate it into answers and solutions...now we are on a journey of mutual and simultaneous exploration. In my view, all we can expect from one another is new and interesting information. We cannot expect answers."

The following, from my observations as a facilitating teacher (mainly while in Position C), are about three students thinking about science as they explore their hypotheses in their own ways. They are preparing for Science Project Day. To start, I asked the students to each plan a project around something they had been wondering about.

Matthew's theories grew as he wrote and illustrated his understanding of how polar bears swim. David wrote to help himself decide about his study of snakes as he thought about the whole reptile family. Kate went about charting her understandings of geese, which she used to guide her study further. The starting point for each of their explorations began with what they knew personally as they worked within their community of learners. I noticed that as they read their writing aloud it was more for their own benefit than for their classmates. The support was indirect — as peers listened they often had another idea.

MATTHEW

Matthew was involved in the process of discovery as he joined his community of learners. He began with his question, "How do polar bears swim?" Every morning, he started with a blank piece of paper. (He used sheets of paper instead of his scribbler because he was planning to make a display of his work to enter the science project day.)

In January, Matthew began to discover the relationships of his world and the bear's world. He didn't try to control his information but rather to experience where his understandings led him as he wrote, illustrated, and shared with his classmates.

Matthew's first decision was to go to the paint center, pin up his blank piece of paper, and paint a polar bear swimming. Later when everyone returned to their circular home base to share their discoveries Matthew told his classmates his bear was swimming for a very important reason. (Children are encouraged to bring their knowing to the blank page before seeking mentors or books. Everyone trusts themselves as learners as they have been

The Polar Bear
iz Swamim
BKas
a Sharc
is Be
hind

him

Figure 6.1a

writing, drawing, and sharing their stories, thoughts, and hypotheses since the first day of school (see chapter 3).) He read his written work, "The polar bear is swimming because a shark is behind him." (See figure 6.1a.)

The next day writing took precedence as Matthew quickly imaged the polar bear with the sun to keep him company. He was busy and preoccupied and didn't share his morning work. He wrote, "Polar bear uses his feet to swim." (See figure 6.1b.)

The next work that Matthew planned to save in his folder was to be placed on a large freestanding cardboard for display day. He wrote, "Polar bear travels in the water because (at) he paddles his feet." (See figure 6.1c.) Then, lying on the floor, he showed how bears move their paws when they are in the water.

In his fourth piece of work, the question, "How do polar bears swim?" appeared to be answered. Matthew wrote, "The polar

Figure 6.1b

Figure 6.1c

The polar Bear swas B kas p v thefr fet.

Figure 6.1d

bear swims because of their feet." (See figure 6.1d.) Matthew incorporated icebergs, which motivated many questions and comments from his peers. For example, one student said that she knew polar bears rested on icebergs when they were tired from swimming.

Matthew continued to work on his own even though the time was right for some of his peers to look in books, build models, or visit an adult. His fifth work included a blue expanse of water with his bear submerged. He shared with a small group and the discussion became intense as the group tried to decide whether a polar bear's enemies were other animals or only humans. Matthew looked through his reports and found one about a polar bear swimming away from a shark. Matthew spent some time finding out about the polar bear's enemies but soon was back with his original topic. He wrote, "The polar bear can go under water so his enemies can't get him." (See figure 6.1e.)

The sixth work reveals Matthew's continued struggle to understand how polar bears swim. At one point he was on the floor

Figure 6.1e

demonstrating how he had pretended to be a polar bear in his bathtub. Many of his peers experimented with him, "swimming" on the floor as they demonstrated their ideas of how bears move in the water. He wrote, "Polar bear the back feet move different directions." (See figure 6.1f.)

We were soon to learn that the bathtub continued to play a part in his search. The seventh work resulted from observing his dog in the bathtub having a bath. Note the bold lines as he gained confidence in his ability to ask questions and solve problems. He wrote, "Polar bears pushes the water with his paws to swim." (See figure 6.1g.)

The eighth work resulted from an interesting turn. Matthew spent some time looking through a zoo magazine about bears (Wexco 1982). One of his peers had brought it to him a few months earlier, but the time to reach for someone else's ideas wasn't until now. He opened the book with a purpose and stopped at the page with the polar bears in the water. In his illustration, the sun reappears, the polar bear is smiling, and the

Figure 6.1f

Figure 6.1g

The drawing contains the handwritten text: "The Polar Bear uossi hes andheBaK Lassy has To Sterar Webb fet"

Figure 6.1h

cloud is whistling. During the sharing everyone was interested and had many comments about the "webbed feet." One student drew a duck's webbed foot on the chalkboard illustrating how the toes were connected by tough skin. Another student brought a Japanese fan to school and explained she thought webbed feet were like the fan. Someone else explained how skin between the toes could help them swim — that was why he kept his fingers closed when he went swimming. Following the discussion, Matthew wrote, "The polar bear uses his back legs to steer and he has webbed feet." (See figure 6.1h.)

The ninth piece of work was truly a breakthrough. The sun appeared very big and yellow and the polar bear continued to

the polar Bear can s
swim
B cais there fr
is water proof

Figure 6.1i

smile. His peers became engaged in wonderful conversation about waterproofing, including someone talking about his dad oiling his boots to waterproof them. This was truly a time for me and any other adults in the classroom to move into Position C and observe the students taking ownership for their own learning. (It's also a time to tuck away new ideas for future lessons; for example, waterproofing.) Matthew wrote, "The polar bear can swim because their fur is waterproof." (See figure 6.1i.)

The tenth work had a cold northern look. Matthew had continued to study his polar bear magazine. Note his name written in full for the first time. He didn't quite finish his last name. He

The Polar Bear Swams Bkas ov wot His poof kot

Matthew R

Figure 6.1j

wrote his name again, after conducting his experiments. By then, he was transferring his knowledge or may have felt he had a clearer understanding how polar bears swim, their natural habitat, and so on. Matthew wrote, "The polar bear swims because of his waterproof coat." (See figure 6.1j.)

The eleventh work included yet another discovery, which he explained orally in great detail using the term *aerodynamics*. Triangles were discussed and drawn everywhere as Matthew and his peers were trying to imagine the abstract simple shape of a polar bear slipping through the water. According to Matthew, the people in the boat above the bear were totally unaware of the ani-

Figure 6.1k

mal's presence. The students loved the mystery. Matthew wrote and shared as he ran to the chalkboard to diagram his understanding of aerodynamics, "The polar bear makes sure no water goes near him because...." (orally he relates) "...he is aerodynamics." (See figure 6.1k.)

DAVID

David sat a few desks away in the circle of learning. He was interested in reptiles and amphibians and had been writing for days and days about them in his scribbler, demonstrating his use of

Figure 6.2: David's original work demonstrates his use of writing as a learning tool for his preplanning.

writing as a learning tool (see figure 6.2). He and his parents were planning a visit to the reptilian section of the zoo to enjoy a personal tour with David's aunt, who worked as a docent. Still, he hadn't shared his ideas or plans for his project and surprisingly hadn't offered any questions or comments in support of his peers. At times, I was tempted to get into his space and find out how he planned to be ready for the display day. I wanted to help him establish his focus. But I resisted. Learning is very personal.

David is an example of a student who chose to work independently. There was no dialogue. At a later point, he wrote several reports on snakes, but always worked independently except the day he gave a talk to the class.

KATE

Kate's work shows yet another way students write to make learning meaningful. She knew what her topic was going to be and how she planned to demonstrate her understanding of it. Her preplans — which she wrote and drew in great detail — revealed she would need eight reports. Each of the eight sections was extended into an eight-page project on geese (see figure 6.3).

STUDENTS NEED TO EXPLORE

Our students need to explore. We, as teachers, must understand this need as a fragile process linking what may appear to be strange paradoxes. Van Manen (1986, 40) says: "Rather than seeing a child's question as something that needs a quick and simple answer, the adult should try to help the child in his or her natural inclination to live the question. I wonder why the sun is so hot? I wonder how the earth was made? I wonder where I came from?" Adults should answer students' questions with questions; students are more likely, then, to live their questions.

Matthew, David, and Kate each made decisions about their learning in a positive nurturing environment where personal wonderings were celebrated within the natural flow of writing, talking, imaging, listening, and growing to trust one's own intuitions.

They each showed their understanding of their question in a unique way. Matthew lived his question independently, with peers, with the zoo magazines and other nonfictional information, in the bathtub, and with his dog. He used talk to learn. He discovered for himself as he built onto his knowing. David was self-directed. He pondered, lingered, and wondered as he wrote to order his learning. Kate, too, was self-directed but used charts, notes, and drawings with clear logical mapping to make sense of her learning.

Figure 6.3: Kate's original work demonstrates her use of charts, mapping, and brief notes to preplan.

Matthew, David, and Kate are examples of how children naturally use their learning styles as they show us how they learn. When we understand what to look for in children, their uniqueness is welcome. They will show us the way!

7

CREATING PLAYS AND MUSIC:
The Learner's Opera

Free play must be tempered with judgment, and judgment tempered with freedom to play...to play freely, we must have a command of technique. Back and forth flows the dialogue of imagination and discipline, passion and precision. We harmonize groundness in daily practice with spiritedness in daily stepping out into the unknown.

– Stephen Nachmanovitch, *Free Play*

This chapter is about a stage of learning in which students demonstrate the lively process of incorporating divergent thinking with serious communication as they create and produce plays and songs with and for their audience. The students practice and produce their creative plays and songs within the community of learners rather than in small groups. The ideas for the productions come from the interests and themes that are going on in the classroom.

After the student has illustrated and webbed his ideas using where, when, who, and what to guide him, he invites some of his peers to be the characters, introduces his play, and introduces each of his characters with an explanation of his part. Each character in turn then explains how he sees himself in the play. The play practice, as well as the production, are played out before the community who are all sitting in the circle. Even the audience is actively involved; they are watching the play unfold as they understood it during the introduction of the plot and characters. At the conclusion of the play the audience may ask questions or make comments to any one of the actors.

The following show how students are supported by their community of learners as they create through art, drama, and song.

KYLA

The spring theme in the first-grade classroom was Hiking with Mother Nature. A mini-theme about dandelions was branching from the main theme and taking shape. Outside, dandelions were bravely flowering along the edges of the school playground at the same time that they were being forced out of the play areas by a fleet of caretakers, armed with poisons and sprays.[1]

Fortunately, the dandelions continued to spring up — and in the most unlikely places. Kyla, one of our resident artists and a self-directed first grader, was able to spend time on-site to compare and verify what authors, poets, and artists had written and illustrated about these hardy plants. She was intrigued with the information she discovered from the pictures, books, task cards, poems, songs, and articles displayed in our classroom nature center. Her interest soared when she saw the drawing of a big dandelion given the powers of a smiling dancer. Karen Teskey, an artist, had spent time in the classroom as a mentor the previous spring and left sketches of dandelions personifying dancing people. (The richness of our theme grows as visitors join the learning and, over the years, have left behind some of themselves.)

As we explored the theme, we enjoyed whole-class lessons about the secrets and strengths of dandelions. Kyla, however, required a longer incubation time to pursue and integrate her ideas without the pressure of closure of these lessons. She quickly

---

[1] This upset me. I question how far we are going to ensure our children are surrounded by only those things that are clipped, neat, and tidy. Will they never experience what it feels like to fall into the deep grass and come face to face with a wee gopher? Or be startled by a curious dragonfly using someone's nose for a landing field? What about the thrill of picking little bouquets of milky dandelions, soft and yellow, for the classroom?

slipped into an individual study. She found a space in the class-room, got help hanging up a large sheet of white paper, and gathered everything that interested her about dandelions from the nature center and from outside. She turned a cardboard box over to serve as a table and it soon overflowed with her projects, poems, and stories. As her ideas took shape she was always ready, at sharing time, to entertain, inform, inspire, and draw together the community of first-grade learners. She painted dan-delions, created hand puppets depicting the dandelion in its three stages of maturity, and wrote and produced a short puppet play for her peers.

The culmination of her study became a synthesis of her learn-ing. She planned a play cleverly incorporating fiction with nonfic-tion, using art (her area of strength) to internalize and transfer her learning. First, she sketched on a large piece of paper to organize the who, when, where, and what of her play.[2]

As she planned her play, she talked and shared with many of her peers. They, in turn, were instrumental in building onto her ideas as her sketches grew in exacting detail on the large paper.

Then, using her sketches, Kyla introduced her play by explain-ing the role of the characters as she envisioned each (who), the time of the big event (when), the place (where), and the problem with a protagonist (what). Each character, in turn, talked about how he saw himself in the play. (For example, the child playing the part of Evil explained that he saw himself perched up on a desk in a space far from the cave and that he would be wearing a black cloak.) The ponies discussed and arrived at a consensus as to where the meadow and the cave would be. Kyla explained her role as Dandelion, the leading character, and assured everyone that they would find out how she solves her problem with Evil.

---

[2] As first graders use the who, when, where, what format to guide their plans for stories or plays, they learn to read and spell these high frequency, low-interest words in a meaningful context. This is one of the numerous ways to ensure that the graphophonemic component of the psycholinguistic model of reading is given stage time equal to the semantics and the syntax in an environ-ment where language is kept whole.

Soon, it was time for her to produce her play. She introduced Dandelion, a girl with long golden locks, who lived in a cave at the edge of the meadow. Here she played with her many little ponies in the sunshine and rested in the evening. The problem was Evil who lurked about trying to kill Dandelion.

The actual presentation of plays is an interesting process in our classroom, as the practicing and celebrating of a play occur simultaneously before the audience. The playwright, Kyla in this instance, invited her characters to the center (see chapter 3) of the community of learners. After decisions were made as to who would be what character (for example, the ponies, Dandelion, and Evil), they quickly grabbed costumes from the trunk full of dress-up clothes. The remaining students assumed the role of an audience with all of its special responsibilities, such as predicting how the problem will be solved.

The audience waited to affirm their predictions. This became a whole-class involvement where the author of the play is guided by encouraging the collaboration of everyone. I enjoyed my role as a facilitating teacher and asked a few guiding questions from the edge (Positions B and C) to help the children build that special awareness of how the input from the characters involved enriches the final production. These included questions about the role of an audience, ways to use space wisely, how to encourage more dialogue, how to make the message clear for the audience, and good versus evil. Any problems to be solved were talked about in the context of what was happening. Kyla experienced the importance of talk as she helped the members of the cast see themselves as part of the decision-making body.

Once the play proceeded, the dialogue and the action (mostly the action) were made clear with a few last-minute directions from Kyla. Her leadership abilities had grown from telling and overpowering to guiding and suggesting. She was coming to understand herself in a social setting. As she orchestrated her play she was learning that everyone couldn't read her mind. The power of talk, motivated by her art, was supported within the hidden structure (not being judgmental, respecting one another's space, and so on) of the community of learners. The students were learning, in a natural setting, to make decisions about their learning, to build onto one another's ideas, and to avoid stepping on anyone's words. These were not rules written on the wall; rather they were lived because Kyla and her peers were engaged in learning. As she shared her experiences and understandings about dandelions through art and drama, Kyla's peers became involved and were supportive yet kept her on her toes.

Kyla was involved personally as she and her peers took risks while making decisions as they constructed knowledge. At the end of the play the audience was invited to ask the cast questions and offer comments. One student asked, "How could you stay alive? When my dad sprayed the dandelions in our yard they died."

Kyla explained, "No matter how many times Evil attacked me I could survive because I'm a whole family of flowers all in one flower."

That led to much discussion about the components of the dandelion — what appears to be one dandelion flower is actually hundreds of flowers. Each flower is complete with a pistil and stamen that can make a seed for a new plant. Ejichi Asayama's book, *Dandelions,* which was in the center, was suddenly charged with new meaning. The microscope and the magnifying glasses were sought after and dandelions found their way to everyone's desk.

The curriculum is made meaningful in strange and wonderful ways as the community of learners make it happen. Egan (1986,35) argues: "it is the unpredictable use, the spontaneity, the creative imagination that is at the educational heart of the matter."

As the teacher, I see my role as a support for the ongoing learning:

◆ by listening

◆ by asking questions that encourage higher-level thinking. Bloom's taxonomy is an excellent guide to help build the themes that integrate the content during the process of learning and to help understand the student's talk in all its diversity. For me, themes have come to be a collection of stuff mainly to have at my fingertips to enrich a teachable moment. (See chapter 4.)

◆ by modeling to promote an insatiable appetite to further ask questions beginning with "how" and "why"

◆ by storying; for example, information found in encyclopedias can be turned into exciting stories

I read stories to weave information with the children's experiences and to foster their natural love of story. However, stories from the children seem to naturally spark learning. Egan (ibid.,47) says: "The educational achievement is not to make the strange seem familiar, but to make the familiar seem strange. It is seeing the wonderful that lies hidden in what we take for granted that matters educationally."

I, too, enjoy writing quickly and sharing just for fun, as it lets me experience being one with my community of learners. When I share, they share their questions and comments about my stories. Writing helps me take off my teacher hat and focus on the storying rather than on mechanics. Many times I just set my story aside remembering that the idea of a community of learners is the children looking within and to each other as they write and talk to learn. The thrill is when I find myself in Position C observing the intensity of self-directed learning.

Kyla's individual project was one of many stories in the community of learners as each student incorporated his interests and familiar knowledge with new discoveries. Kyla, making sense of her learning through talk, was celebrated during the exciting daily drama that unfolded as each student saw himself as an intricate part of the community of learners. As Douglas Barnes (1992, 14) explains:

> To become meaningful a curriculum has to be enacted by pupils as well as teachers....By 'enact' I mean come together in a meaningful communication — talk, write, read books, collaborate, become angry with one another, learn what to say and do and how to interpret what others say and do...

Kyla and her peers, as they talked, drew, listened, wrote, read books, and argued, were highly engaged in committing facts to memory, reasoning and enjoying the discovery that her dandelions could survive the sprays, depicted by Evil wearing a black cloak. Actions and talk enabled the children to grow and change as learning about dandelions followed many direction. One topic, the environmental issue concerning sprays used on playgrounds, was discussed among the parents and letters were written to modify this practice.

A KINDERGARTEN CLASS

One wintry day a few weeks before Christmas the children in my kindergarten class and I found ourselves responsible for a production in the upcoming Christmas concert. This little community of learners had been involved in making their learning decisions, so I knew they would find it strange if the plans for their concert came from a book or from me.

I sat down for an important chat with them. "It is almost time for our Christmas concert. How do you see yourself in a Christmas concert?" Without a moment's hesitation Lynsey replied, "I am Mrs. Santa and I say 'Welcome' to all the children that are here!" It was as if the floodgates had opened. Talk poured through my big blue felt pen and I charted as fast as I could to catch the talk.

Mark's little black eyes sparkled as he exclaimed, "I am Santa and I check my list and I bring toys to the kids."

Zane began to act out his part. "Hello, I am Rudolph. I guide Santa's sleigh."

Beth, our artist, ran for some paper and began drawing a big woolly sheep. She later shared, "I sing, 'The sheep lay down, the sheep lay down, by the cradle.'"

Ben, who rarely spoke, surprised everyone when he talked about the colored lights. He enjoyed the stories about lights from his peers before he crafted his speaking part. "I make your house beautiful with all the colored lights." He decided to be a Christmas tree decorated with lights.

There was little doubt in Merissa's mind as she took my pen and sketched an angel at the top of the chart paper, "I am the angel. I brought the baby to the kids."

Taya, who sees her world of learning through music, quietly said, "I will be sleeping in the cradle and pop up and sing." She then began singing *Away in a Manger* with perfect pitch.

To anyone happening by, the chart paper looked like meaningless scratches, but to us it was the essence of our concert taking shape.

I asked the students if they could draw a large picture of how they envisioned their appearance. It was then that Chelsea, who hadn't shared her part in the play, said, "I will be the rabbit. I will help kids find a tree out in the forest."

The talk continued as each student filled a large piece of plain white paper with ideas of how he would be dressed for the grand occasion, which we called Christmas as We See It.

The following day we toured the gym and saw the stage in a new light, then returned to the classroom for a whole-class discussion. As they focused for a chalk talk to encourage mind mapping, I took the lead, like a coach might do before a football game. I drew a rectangle on the chalkboard to represent the gym and arranged the symbol O into rows to stand for the parents sitting in the audience. Then on the stage I scattered a few Xs to stand for the students in the production.

Students' drawings of what they will look like when they are dressed up for the Christmas play.

Students practice the play (with puppets representing themselves) on the miniature stage.

I encouraged everyone to make standup puppets of themselves. I crafted a big cardboard box into a miniature stage with pull curtains. As each puppet was finished the children discussed and enacted their space on stage in relation to each other, their movements, and where the cradle, our only prop, would be located. Everyone knew their lines after the first discussion, and their positions on stage. By using puppets to enact the play on the miniature stage in the classroom for days before the big night, everyone had a clear mind map that transferred to the actual stage long before the event. The fun practices with the puppets, which were instigated by the children, were a natural way for shy children to learn to project their voice.

When the children decided that following Taya's song at the end they would all join together to sing the song again and ask the audience to join, I knew these students had truly taken ownership of their production.

Figure 7.1: *The children are used to seeing their telling, drawing, and temporary spelled stories written conventionally, then glued beside their original story. However, Juan had not invented a way to save the original of his musical story. Later, he got help from the music teacher who wrote the notes as he hummed the tune he wanted.*

JUAN

Juan, a first-grader with a passion for wars and guns, joined his community of learners in September. He drew pictures of guns firing and bombs exploding. Using his detailed drawings, he explained how guns were made. He mapped and used an original system of symbols (a "Juan special") to illustrate his stories about troops, their survival, and take-over strategies. He studied as well as created intricate maneuvers used on land, sea, and air.

As I observed this highly mathematical- and logical-minded child, I wondered how I could help him see war as something less than exciting. As my colleagues and I talked, we reminded ourselves that school must be a place for students to talk, experiment, and discover all sides of an issue, enabling them to make wise choices and decisions.

One day Juan began to share his ideas of the suffering he viewed on the televised news. His stories began taking a turn toward nonviolence. He seemed more interested in how to solve the problems in different ways.

Then came a story, illustrated on a diorama. A flat box was covered with submarines, tankers, fighter jets, and soldiers all with a purpose. He told the story in song, making up the words as he sang. He captivated the class, not to mention me. Everyone wanted to sing with him. So we charted the words, rearranging a few phrases with the help of his peers so that it would flow. It was typed and everyone was given a copy. (Reasons to read always find a way under the main spotlight in my classroom.)

The next discussion focused on a way to sing Juan's tune with consistency. I shared some of the techniques used by musicians such as tempo, high sounds, low sounds, and a symbol system called notes used to save songs. Juan knew exactly how the tune sounded, and I was relieved when the music teacher, whom the students visited twice a week, offered to listen to their humming and singing and model how to use musical notes to save their sounds (see figure 7.1).

* * *

I was recently talking to Barbara Bridges, the librarian at the Centre for Gifted Education at the University of Calgary. She handed me a book review of Rena Upitis's book *Can I Play You My Song?* "This sounds like a book you'd be interested in, Anne." In the review, Carl Braun writes that in the world of music children "construct their systems before the systems others have constructed will make sense." In other words, they know when it is time to reach for conventional notation and the work constructed by others in music just as they know when to reach for the conventional alphabet and the stories written by accomplished authors. Needless to say I was off to find Rena Upitis's books *Can I Play You My Song?* and *This Too Is Music*. I found myself reading half the night away. The books were not written when I was searching for ways to facilitate Juan's learning. They now have become a vital part of my professional library so that I am able to observe those teachable moments as children continue to naturally incorporate music into their learning. Many children discover they can use musical notes to write music stories just as they use the alphabet to write word stories.

* * *

The opera within an opera is never ending as our young students, making their learning meaningful through art, drama, and music, lead us to revisit our knowing, and to read about the experiences of master teachers.

8
STUDENT
SELF-EVALUATION:
Folios Kept
in the Port

We expect too little from the students, take too much on ourselves. In this way we lose valuable opportunities to find out what
purposes and possibilities students bring to the classroom, where
they need help — and where they could offer guidance to us as
their teachers.

– James Britton, *Language and Learning*

STUDENT-LED INTERVIEWS

There is a yellow table just outside the circle of desks in
our classroom. One of many things that happens
around the table is student-led interviews. The young
student wiggles onto a chair and relishes his parents'
undivided attention. Each interview takes an interesting direction
of its own, as what is important to each child is emphasized. The
interview may also include a tour of the gym, a detailed descrip-
tion of the problem solving that takes place in the sandbox, viewing special paintings from the portable bulletin board, readings
from a book, or singing a favorite song from a chart on the wall.

Each child shares one or two of the above-mentioned activities
and his scribbler full of stories. These reveal a clear picture of the
child's developmental stage in the reading/writing process. The
work samples on pages 112-116 show five-year-old Echo's
gradual and natural development over the course of a year.

Figure 8.1: This story shows the illustrations and scribbling stage. Echo was telling her story as she followd her scribbles and drawings.

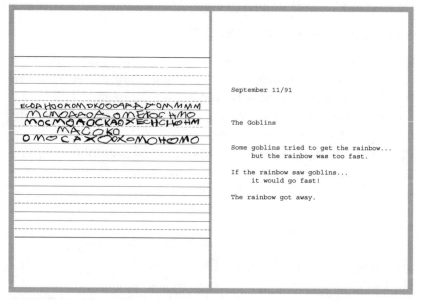

Figure 8.2: Note the letter-like forms as Echo strings them together to represent her writing.

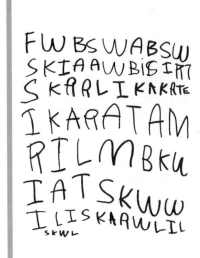

FW BS WABSW
SKIAAWBISIAT
S KAALI KAKATE
I KARATAM
RILMBKU
IATSKWW
I LISKAAWLIL
skwl

October 7/91

The Fog

I went walking to the gate.
    I saw fog!

I saw the school bus.
    I went on the bus.

I rode to school.
    I like the bus ride.

Figure 8.3: This story shows Echo's use of letters and early word/symbol relationships such as "skwl" for school.

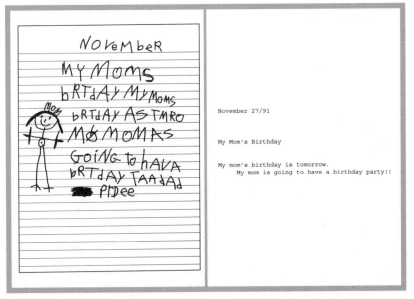

NOveMbeR

MY MoMS
bRTdAY MYMoMS
bRTdAY AS TMRO
MØ MoM AS
GoiNG to hAVA
bRTdAY TAAdAd
    PrDee

November 27/91

My Mom's Birthday

My mom's birthday is tomorrow.
    My mom is going to have a birthday party!!

Figure 8.4: Here, Echo shows she understands sound/symbol relationships as she moves from speech to print. She is using temporary selling as well as some conventionally spelled words.

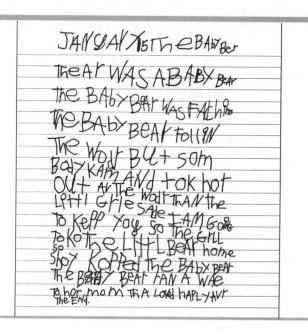

January 15/92

The Baby Bear

There was a baby bear.
The baby bear was fishing.
The baby bear fell in the water
     but somebody came out and took her out of the water.
Then the little girl said, "I am going to keep you."
So the little girl took the little bear home.
     She kept the baby bear.
The baby bear ran away to her mom.
They lived happily ever after.
THE END

Figure 8.5: By January, Echo is leaving spaces between her words. Over half her words are conventionally spelled.

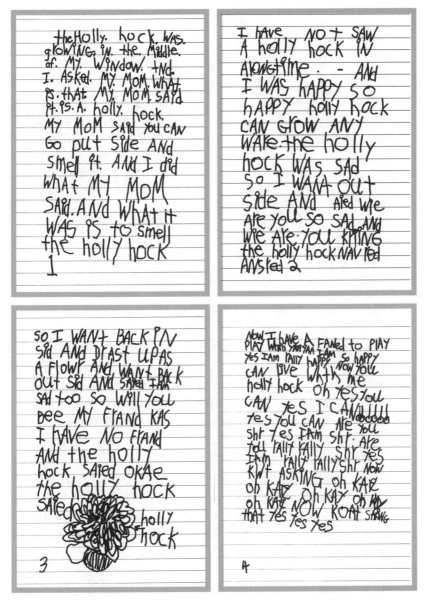

Figure 8.6: By March, Echo is comfortable making the alphabet work for her as she writes. She can pay more attention to the storyline — The Hollyhock has a beginning, middle, and an ending — as the sound/symbol relationships have become more automatic. (See page 125 for translation.)

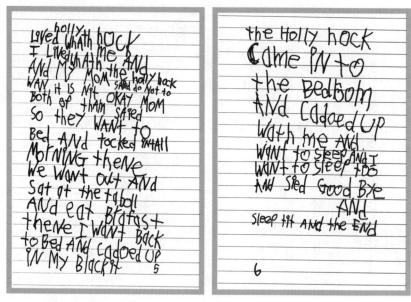

Figure 8.6 (cont'd)

Student-led interviews, beginning in kindergarten, open the doors for teachers and parents to observe children in a very honored setting. Teachers observe students taking responsibility for their learning as they share what is important to them. Parents are able to step back and watch their children "rise to the occasion." We gain privileged information from the student's point of view. The interview builds onto the information from the anecdotal report card (which reports the student's progress as a learner in relation to himself and his learning in relation to the curriculum) and helps us to understand the student's zone of proximal development. This is the zone between what a child can do independently and what he can accomplish with help. It is important to find a child's zone of proximal development because, as Orin and Donna Cochrane (1992,27) point out: "Learning activities in the zone of proximal development allow the child to build on and expand his/her knowledge."

The day of the interviews arrives. Each family, in turn, finds a place around the yellow table. This sturdy little table with peeling

One mother's reflections on her son's student-led interview

At our Parent/Teacher conference, Mrs. Green showed us Ty's file and some of his work, then she asked him if he would like to share any of it with us. Ty grasped the sheets and started reading the stories aloud to us. He was following his own printed words and would come to a word he didn't recognize and would automatically start sounding out his letters and would get through the word and on to the next one. His father's face was lighting up with a proud smile, and our eyes exchanged a silent, "Heh — our little guy is doing great. He's actually reading."

Next Ty was sharing a report he had done on barn swallows. Instead of Mrs. Green handing us his finished report and poster and showing us his work, Ty was given the opportunity to tell us about his completed research. He showed us all the information he had collected and mounted on a sheet of paper, along with a model clay nest he had built at school to represent a swallow's real nest.

At home we had witnessed the beginnings of the swallow project taking shape. When I asked him what he was going to learn about swallows, he answered he didn't know exactly. Next thing I see my supper preparations come to a halt as he shows me a list he has made. He had drawn several pictures in a column. Each, he told us, represented information he wanted to find out for himself. For example: he had drawn a camera, meaning he wanted to take a picture of a swallow; he had drawn a picture of a dish, meaning he wanted to find out what they ate for food; he had drawn a tape recorder, meaning he wanted to try to tape their voices, and so on. All of this was really getting him excited. To see your child's face light up is always pleasing to a parent, but to see your child that excited when they are talking about their school project or the theme topic they are working on is even more rewarding. He didn't want to do anything but work on this project. "Mom, can you get the camera down off the shelf? Mom, can I get the tape recorder from the living room? Dad, do we have a really long extension cord I can use?"

Whether the picture would turn out or not I had no idea, and whether he would be able to catch their voices on tape I was unsure. He worked on this on and off after school for at least a week, always with the same enthusiasm. He fed them oats and hid behind the shed, and did eventually get their tiny peeping voices along with some howling wind and the sound of some trucks driving by.

When he shared at the Parent/Teacher conference he was very proud of his own work. We know he came out of the experience with an abundance of knowledge on swallows...not because the teacher had read out of a textbook and given a lesson on the swallow, but because he was allowed to choose his own avenue of research, that being, as much hands-on research as written material. While he was having fun, we could see that he was learning from his actual experiences.

To go to your interview and have your child want you to be there and be so excited about showing you his accomplishments, leaves you with a feeling of satisfaction and pride. The atmosphere at the Parent/Teacher conference was relaxed, giving us the parents, Ty, and the teacher time and space to express feelings. Even the areas where Ty needed extra assistance were discussed, all being easily related in this team atmosphere of parent-child-teacher.

paint, which I retrieved from the garbage truck, is treated with great respect as visiting teachers, parents, and dignitaries, interested in observing a community of learners in action, come to our room.

In one student-led interview, a student proudly turning each page of his prized scribbler, read stories with beginnings, middles, and endings. He often stopped to remind his parents of the names of the letters that he had scattered among his drawings. He asked for help with some of the letters' sounds, which indicated one zone of proximal development for him. He ended his interview by drawing an elaborate design with interlocking circles. As he finished he explained the pattern, "The bottom ones go this way [horizontal]. The middle ones stand up [vertical] and the top ones go like the bottom ones [horizontal]." He then slipped off to the sand table and left his parents and I smiling at each other. We spoke briefly of how his attention span appeared to be so short in the classroom but of how he had demonstrated, in this interview, the parts of the curriculum he had mastered or was ready to learn with help. I told them that he was spending increased time each morning writing, drawing, sharing, listening, and talking with his classmates.

During these interviews, I constantly gain new insight into how each child transfers learning. I find the students confidently share their understandings. There is no planning ahead. I just ask each student, as he settles in with his parents at the yellow table, to talk about his favorite part of school. When the interview seems to be at an end I ask him if he has any concerns or problems that we might be able to help solve. The interview unfolds naturally. The proof of the pudding is a child spontaneously sharing (or not sharing) how he sees himself in the context of the learning.

PORTFOLIOS

There are many good books written about evaluation (I list some in the bibliography). One effective way to evaluate and share

learning is through student portfolios. With portfolios, we are encouraged to keep the whole child in mind, taking care not to shift
our attention to the parts.

Tierney et al. (1991,70) stress: "portfolios lose their effectiveness if they are institutionalized. We use the term *institutionalize*
to refer to the use of portfolios in terms spelled out by outsiders. If
students lose control of their own work, portfolios become just
another assignment."

Perrone (1991,166) points out: "assessment needs to go beyond most current testing technologies if schools are to be powerful educational settings...assessment should empower students
as learners. In fact, the kinds of assessment activities that are
authentic — the portfolios, documentation, and exhibitions...for
example — contribute importantly to student self-evaluation."

I often look through the students' portfolios to find the most
recent sample of their printing (which usually bears little resem-
blance to the writing they use to save their stories.) I might find

◆ a sheet of math problems indicating how a student uses
   strategies for solving math problems (see figure 2.1, page 32)

◆ a story a student has read silently or had read for him, accompanied by a synopsis, partly written, mostly illustrated, but
   that can be easily brought to life by the oral retelling

◆ stories consisting of pages of temporary spellings or strings of
   letters, but with detailed illustrations that say more than
   words ever could. (These stories are accompanied by a typed
   copy, conventionally spelled, which are passed out to the
   author's classmates during formal reading and sharing time.
   See chapter 3.)

◆ pieces of art, revealing in great detail, the student's passion
   (for example, dogs, horses, dinosaurs, dragons, unicorns,
   snakes, or queens)

As I sit reflecting about each student, I often make notes. For
example:

Jackie: So delighted with her discovery of how to make the alphabet work for her that she carries her scribbler everywhere, even to the playground.

Sergei: Rewriting math problems, incorporating twists that challenge him. It isn't important that the 5 is reversed for he has higher-level concepts to consider and reconsider at this point in his learning. He never complains of being bored.

Ross: The sketchy farm story that he presented to his community of learners, the rich questioning that it motivated and his ability to think, explain, and defend as he stood before his peers. He suddenly became distant, so unlike him, as he said, "I am going to write three new parts to add to my story. I'll tell you later." The second story was handed out, read by everyone, and shared. Ross captivated everyone's attention. This time even Jackie put her pen down (remember, during informal sharing time, writing may continue, but no talking (see chapter 3).)

Ross's story went into great detail about finding $10,000 on the west farm and how he gave so many thousands to each member of his family. According to his calculations he would have $900.00 left for himself.

As the story ended, Ronnie was out of his desk, inviting the students to check Ross's calculations concerning the sharing of the $10,000.

He held up his hands, "Say each of my fingers were $1000.00." He then curled up one finger each time $1000.00 was given away. Following a lively debate with many side conversations and a chalkboard full of numbers with lots of zeros, the consensus of the class was that Ross would have $1900.00 left rather than $900.00. Ross was the catalyst involving the community of learners in some heavy-duty thinking. Ross's interpersonal talent is definitely in his favor.

Autumn: Shyly finding me to share a sentence tucked into her five-page story. "Listen to this. I especially like this word. Don't you, Mrs. Green?" She is writing to please herself; a self-directed learner.

Josh: Announcing a day or two ago, "Listen to me flow when I read." His decision to invite me to hear his accomplishments. He was very surprised when he brought his chicken to school and, while lying beside its cage as he wrote his story, discovered the sounds it was making: "c-l-u-c-k."

Ty: Working on his most recent independent study about barn swallows, reading nonfiction, writing reports, displaying his diagrams and drawings. To demonstrate the real nest of the swallows in his barn at home, he made a nest of mud. To top it off he played his tape of the swallows chirping in his barn.

To be successful, however, evaluation must be a student-led process. The focus is to help students understand themselves as learners as they take responsibility in the evaluation process. In our high-tech, rapidly changing world, it is more important than ever for our young people to be able to communicate vital questions and solutions. They must be able to demonstrate their expertise and explain what they can bring to the whole.

The young students who sit comfortably around the yellow table in my classroom talk without hesitation about their learning as they see it. It is our responsibility, as parents and teachers, to make a mental note of each child's zone of proximal development so that we can find the teachable moments to help that student help himself.

A classic interview occurred one evening as Aven sat gingerly between her mother and father. Aven read her farm story along with several others with a similar sequencing format. Her mother looked at me, "Is it usual that they write 'I this, I that, I...' over and over again?" I explained she was experimenting with all aspects of the reading and writing process. She was demonstrating a desire to create meaning through print; however, the mechanics of printing and spelling had become her focus. This limited her use of language and her stories appeared to have stopped at the stage Applebee calls "sequences" — when a student lists in order what he has done that day (see figure 8.7).

Before any more was said Aven slipped off to her desk and began to write. In her mind her part in the interview was over.

As her parents and I continued to talk I learned that Aven's mother was going over her written stories and helping her to spell her words conventionally. Also they were choosing only books at the library with limited vocabulary so that Aven could read them. Her parents and I discussed the dangers of overemphasizing spelling at this point in Aven's writing development. I told them she must be free to use her writing to experiment with her use of language, enjoy using big words temporarily spelled, and to discover the sounds of the alphabet in a meaningful context as they fall off the end of her pencil. We also discussed that reading good literature would provide models to help Aven find her sense of story. The trips to the library to find easy reading material must include an abundance of good literature.

At that point, Aven popped back to read us what she had been writing (see figure 8.8).

Aven led the way for her parents to understand how the writing/reading process will naturally balance the graphophonemics and syntax of our language with the semantics, and for her teacher to appreciate Vygotsky's zone of proximal development in action.

A fifteen-minute interview left Aven, her parents, and me with that special feeling that comes with self-discovery. The timing was right, with a little help, to build onto her parents' understanding of short sentences all beginning with "I." It *is* possible when a student leads.

When the evaluation process is led by those who know best — our students — they will say confidently, "I'm the one in charge of celebrations" (Baylor 1986, 2). No rehearsals are necessary.

Sometimes I wonder how I can share with parents just how special their child is as he begins that personal journey to life-long learning. The reflections are never ending.

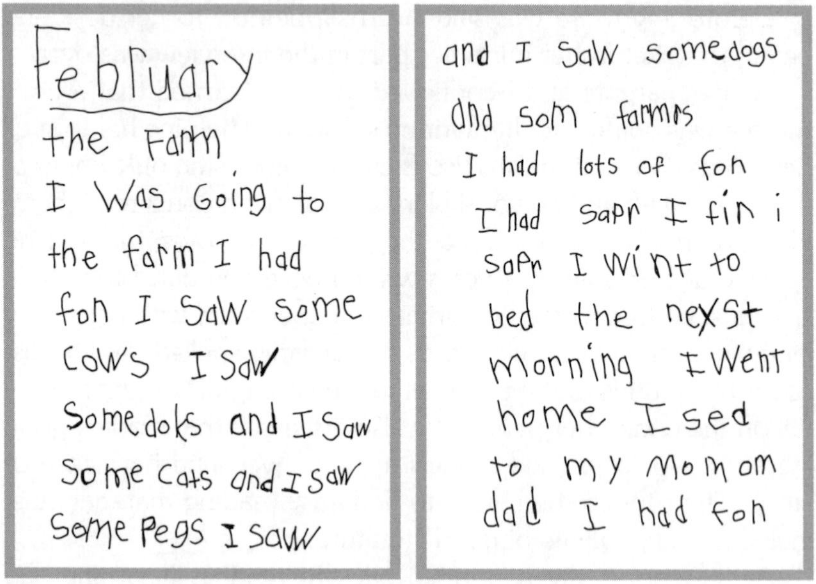

February
the Farm
I Was Going to
the farm I had
fon I Saw some
cows I Saw
Some doks and I Saw
So me Cats and I Saw
Some Pegs I Saw

and I Saw some dogs
and som farmrs
I had lots of fon
I had sapr I fin i
sapr I wint to
bed the nexSt
morning I Went
home I sed
to my mo m om
dad I had fon

Figure 8.7: Aven's farm story, which shows sequencing.

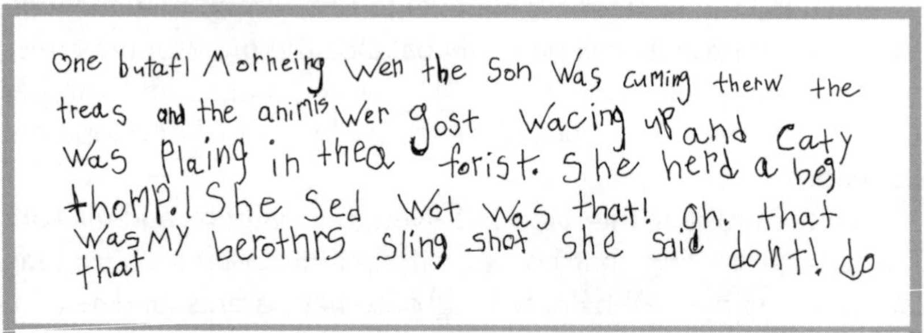

One butafl Morneirg Wen the Son Was cuming therw the
treas and the aninils Wer gost Wacing up and Caty
Was Plaing in thea forist. She herd a beg
thomp. I She Sed Wot Was that! Oh. that
Was MY berothrs sling shot she said dont! do
that

> One beautiful morning when the sun was
> coming through the trees and the animals
> were just waking up and Caty was playing
> in the forest she heard a big thomp! She
> said, "What was that? Oh, that was my
> brother's sling shot." She said, "Don't
> do that!"

Figure 8.8: Aven's story that she wrote at her interview (top) and the typed copy (below).

Translated Copy of *The Hollyhock*

March 24/92

The Hollyhock

The hollyhock was growing in the middle of my window.
I asked my mom, "What is that?"
My mom said, "It is a hollyhock."
My mom said, "You can go outside and smell it."
And I did what my mom said.
And what it was is to smell the hollyhock.

———

I have not seen a hollyhock in a long time.
And I was happy. So happy!!
Hollyhocks can grow anywhere.
The hollyhock was sad.
So I went outside and said, "Why are you so sad? And why are you crying?"
The hollyhock never answered.

———

So I went back inside and dressed up as a flower.
And went back outside and said, "I am sad too, so will you be my friend cause
I have no friends?"
And the hollyhock said, "Okay," The hollyhock said,

———

"Now I have a friend to play with. Yeah! Yeah! I am so happy. Yes I am really
happy."
"Now you can live with me hollyhock. Oh yes you can."
"Yes I can!!"
"Yes you can."
"Are you sure?"
"Yes, I am sure."
"Are you really, really sure?"
"Yes, I am really, really sure. Now quit asking."
"Okay, okay, okay, okay, okay."
"Now quit saying that."
"Yes, yes, yes."

———

The hollyhock lived with me
and I lived with the hollyhock.
And my mom said, "Do not talk when it is night."
"Okay mom," both of them said.
So they went to bed and talked until morning.
Then we went out and sat at the table and ate breakfast.
Then I went back to bed and cuddled up in my blanket.

———

The hollyhock came into the bedroom and cuddled up with me and went to sleep.
And I went to sleep too. And said, "goodbye and sleep tight."
And the end.

9
PARENTS
AS PARTNERS:
Melt in with
the Learning

Education should be the process of helping everyone to discover his uniqueness, to teach him how to develop that uniqueness, and then to show him how to share it because that's the only reason for having anything.

– Leo Buscaglia, *Living, Loving and Learning*

THE ROLE OF PARENTS

Over the years, as more and more parents joined the community of learners and the excitement of educational change became a reality, I was encouraged to explore many dimensions of learning. Parents stopped saying, "But I can't write," and began to write with their children. Some wrote stories, poetry, or songs to share their expertise and passions while others wrote to make sense of their child's learning environment, so different from their own. Many published their writing in our school newspaper for all parents to read as well as for those in the community beyond the school.

So, what *is* the role of the parent in a community of learners? This is what one mother wrote.

My first thought is, for myself, that the parent needs a complete desire to be involved and to want to do this. Whatever this is.

To be interested and to want to know the answer to the question — how do they learn? That would be the first role. Without a desire then I have to conclude it should be hard to do this. From this desire comes the interest, then comes a commitment, then comes self-satisfaction.

From a desire would come a role. What is a role — a model, a director, an observer, a space giver, a helper, a manager? Perhaps all these things. I don't know.

To me this is not a "school." It is a friendly warm building where big kids and little kids come to help and have fun, to experience, to enjoy, *to discover each other*, to experiment, to expand, to share, to grow, and to want things in life.

For myself it is an experience. I did not get all of the above when I went to school.

As parents continue through the stages of learning, they, like their children, question and wonder in their struggle to understand change. Parents' past training and experience with education make it challenging for them to trust what they intuitively know should be the guiding factors for their child's education — his strengths and talents. Instead, they often feel pressured to have their child's success measured in ways similar to when they went to school. Although it seems easier to continue to organize learning into small measurable bites that are committed to the short-term memory for the sake of a mark, that does not build a firm foundation for life-long learning — for example, the isolated weekly spelling list. Instead, I have children compile personal lists, which consist of words from their daily writing in all subject areas. These are words they need to learn to spell conventionally. Each child's list is different.

I have had the privilege of watching children easily forget themselves and show me how they see the world. One time, a student spontaneously remarked, as he wrote the number "4," "Look, teacher, if you put a line here and a curve here it could be a piece of a puzzle." I put aside my first response — a reminder to pay attention to the way "4" is written, and what the word represents — and listened to his explanation. I noticed his mother looking at the child beside him, who was writing "4," consistently moving along adding and subtracting numerals that equal "4" to demonstrate his understanding of the concept of the numeral. I explained about the spatial style of learning, and about how students with this style enjoy drawing their ideas. I shared how Picasso saw a nose when his teacher wrote "4" on the chalkboard and found himself filling in the rest of the details of a face (which demonstrated his spatial style of learning).

Parents involved in a community of learners with their children soon realize that learning is not about comparing one child to another, but about how children build onto one another's ideas while they actually build onto their personal learning.

When parents visit my classroom, I encourage them to bring their younger children with them. At first, many are reluctant to do so. They worry their child will talk aloud and interrupt the class (the students are involved in learning and only become anxious if we become anxious). I tell them that everyone, including a younger child, is a part of the community of learners and that talk is an integral part of learning. They soon learn to relax when their young child utters his talking sounds. It is up to us to prevent learning, in the school setting, from becoming isolated from real life (see chapter 1, Why Do Babies Cry? Why Do People Cry?). I have noticed how easily children carry their scribbler from home to school on the first day of grade one when they have experienced joining the community of learners as a preschooler. This is the case even when both parents with full-time jobs can only manage to come to the classroom once a month.

Parents who join their children at school do more than cut and paste, photocopy, or cook for the students. They *experience* the direction education must take to support their children in the twenty-first century. They see firsthand that the basics, including phonics, provide a meaningful support for students as they make decisions about their learning. They learn firsthand the importance of educational change. They become interested in radio and televised talk shows and newspaper articles about whole lan-

Parents as Facilitators: One Mother's Story

As our seven year old came to the supper table, I asked him how his farm story was coming along.

"I got it started," he said quietly.

"How does it start?"

"One stormy..." he replied.

That was a start all right, I thought. Suppressing my urge to say "Is that all?" I tried to think of something positive.

"What a great beginning, " I said. "Was it day or night?"

From that simple question, a conversation started in which the whole family became involved, asking questions and giving suggestions to our little author. Our three-year-old made up his own "one stormy" story and "wrote" about it in his notebook. (He has a scribbler just like his older brother's in which he can draw or write stories.)

By the time supper was over, our seven-year-old's head was brimming with ideas to continue his story the next day and we, as a family, had had a wonderful time of creative interaction. I realized that by accident and just by knowing a little of what was going on in the classroom, we had come across an avenue for home communication.

guage, phonics, and report cards. It is exciting when parents share a book, an article, or a concern about recent media coverage on education with me.

Parents' questions and sharing are the foundation for change in our schools of the future. I have had the good fortune to build onto my learning because of their questions and sharing. Over the years, we have read and discussed articles and books that have encouraged and helped us understand the importance of giving students the opportunity to show us the way. We soon realize that by seeing the way through the eyes of the student we can ask the question or give help without taking the learning away.

Unfortunately, all too often, as parents, our insight and comprehension of our child's day at school is reduced to something like:

"What happened at school today?"

"Umm, nothin' much."

"Did you learn anything?"

"Yeah."

"Good. Hang up your coat please."

There are many rewards for family members who learn together and nurture one another's unique learning style. I recently read an education column in our daily newspaper stressing that our students' futures ride on what they do in a two-hour exam. A tutor warns: "You can change a love of learning into getting things down and spitting them out." But, I wonder, would we even need tutors for our children if family members learned together and nurtured one another's learning style?

As parents become facilitators and guides in their home, children continue to be self-motivated, enthusiastic, and comfortable with change, uncertainty, and setbacks just as they were as preschoolers. Parents have shared with me that their family life has been enriched since they began using the questioning strategies they observed while being a part of their child's community of learners in the classroom. At home, they now ask questions rather than tell, thus encouraging their children to be a part of the decision making. Even young members of the family take charge when parents ask questions such as, "How do you see it?" and "What do you have to do to get the job done?" Children need to take charge of their affairs. It may appear disorganized to us as adults. Then again we have to be aware of the various learning styles within any one family. Dr. Thomas Armstrong has written two books[1] that leave parents smiling and saying, "Oh yes, now I understand why my child goes about his world differently than we do."

---

[1] *In Their Own Way: Discovering and Encouraging Your Child's Personal Learning Style* and *Seven Kinds of Smart: Identifying and Developing Your Many Intelligences*

Reading material on parent-school relationships can be found in our bookstores and on magazine shelves. It outlines the past relationships and reasons for change. The traditional family, where one parent works to support the needs and one parent remains at home to care for the children is no longer the norm. Today, single-parent families, families with two parents working outside the home, and families from many different ethnic backgrounds and attitudes about schooling have children coming together in one school. It is time for parents and teachers to see themselves in a partnership role, to engage in more meaningful communication, and to have a voice regarding money, pedagogy, and even staff. Joining the community of learners in the classroom to experience storying with teachers and children might be the connection parents need to truly weave partnerships with understanding from the inside out. Schooling is about children, so it makes sense to reacquaint ourselves with learning through their eyes.

We must redefine learning — as one mother did when she entered her child's classroom the week prior to the science fair. Her daughter was about to find a spot on her crowded science board for another picture of her horse. The pencil sketches and stories with temporary spelling and curled edges were not colored or mounted on colored paper. The aesthetics, as we as adults understand, were not important to this student who had spent weeks passionately using her experiences to discover what she knew.

Her mother told me:

I was immediately caught up in the excitement of the day. My daughter proudly showed me her science board. Suddenly all the wonderful ideas and methods that I had been trying to absorb since September flew out the window! From the hidden depths of my own schooling came this horrible, conventional, critical woman, who began to organize my child's project. A few tears later (on both sides) and a long talk with you, I joined the community of learners. The finished product is not the idea; the learning and reaching throughout the project is. May schooling and life become one science fair project after another for these wonderful young people.

I have parents join the learning long after their child graduates from first grade. They slip into my classroom to write, and before leaving remark "I just needed to rethink what was important again." Parents from all walks of life soon come to know, as they experience sharing their story in a community of learners, how naturally their children in inclusive classrooms are enriched as they build onto one another's ideas. Everyone has a story. Dr. Jean Clandinin[2] shared: "the greatest risk is if I silence myself and the stories go untold. Stories are a part of the circle of dialogue that help us to understand ourselves."

If we — teachers, parents, and children — come together as partners we will help one another understand what the current methods about children and learning are and live with them for the sake of the children.

The secrets that support imaginative and caring partnerships can be discovered as we join our children in their community of learners, then let go and share stories. Our stories help us, as we debate our concerns for education, to step back and think about learning in the larger context of wholeness. Our stories encourage us to experience education as living, breathing, and changing so that we learn with our environment rather than about it. Learning with a community of learners enables us to grow with the strength of a plant that pushes away a stone. But, this is a process in which we, as parents and teachers, must be patient for we often try to hurry our children when they aren't yet ready.

---

[2] Dr. Clandinin gave the keynote address, entitled *Stories of Possibility,* at the 1994 Early Childhood Education Council Conference.

Parents as partners is about empowering our children as we journey with them to become aware of what it means to help them help themselves. At home, in the classroom, or at parent meetings, the journey becomes continuous.

10
LEADERSHIP
IS THE KEY:
The Program
Becomes the Person

We know that the best way to build ownership is to give over the creation process to those who will be charged with its implementation.

– Margaret J. Wheatley, *Leadership and the New Science*

People with leadership qualities have the ability to differentiate the roles of the various players so that each functions in an area of strength. Leadership is about empowerment.

Within the school building, the principal is the leader. The effectiveness of her leadership is measured by her ability to stretch each staff member's ability to work with students. Everyone has a role to play — the teaching and nonteaching staff, the students, the parents, the community at large, the school trustees, and "central office" staff all make up a piece of the puzzle. Each group has a major role at specific times although its members may change depending on the complexity of the task being dealt with. The role of the principal complements the learning that goes on in the school by capitalizing on the strength of each of the community members. The focus may be on students, other staff members within the building, the curriculum, timetables, or even external matters that relate to the school. The facilitation of each group's purpose is a precise skill that flows from the belief system and vision of the principal. Many are able to steer the staff through stormy times, initiate change, keep parents involved and on side, and have full cooperation from central office. Unfortunately, many others are unable to facilitate the growth of the staff, partially paralyzing the effectiveness of the school in meeting the needs of the students.

Why, then, are some successful, while others are not? It appears those who are successful share a couple of important characteristics: confidence in their own leadership abilities and faith in the abilities of their staff and students.

THE KEY TO CHANGE

The principal is the key to change. But to implement changes, she must also be an intuitive person with a vision of where she is going. Her energies must inspire all members to make a difference for students. And there must be a philosophy. This is created by students, teachers, support staff, and parents; the slogan from the Community School Movement[1] during the 1970s and 1980s — "Everyone a teacher, everyone a learner!" — sums up this philosophy. It is the rudder that keeps us on course while the vision provides us with the goal toward which we are traveling. Still, there is no point developing a philosophy of change if it is just going to be stowed away. This is why it is so important to adjust the delivery system — how we teach — in our schools rather than adjust the students. One way we can do this is through school-wide evaluation or teacher assessment. Each principal has her own way of doing this (for example, checklists, peer observation, script writing followed by teacher/evaluator dialogue). By collaborating, we can work toward a common ob-

---

[1] The Community School Movement was based on the premise that many of the curriculum skills and concepts could be better taught through community issues using community resource people rather than isolating the curriculum from real life. The main focus was to bring reality to the curriculum rather than learning facts in isolation.

jective — restructuring the delivery system so that our students are actively involved in their own learning.

Striving to increase the level of independence in our students must be preceded by an increase in the level of independence of the teachers, which, in turn, is preceded by increasing the level of independence of our school administration. The increased emphasis on site-based management at the school level (for example, the money allocated to operate the school becomes the responsibility of the principal and her staff) is the beginning of this independence.

BECOMING A COMMUNITY OF LEARNERS

In my school, we experienced becoming a community of learners as we designed, molded, and remolded our interpretation of the philosophy for our school. That philosophy became the guide to meaningful conversations.

In the initial stages change occurred in isolated pockets. But as we saw change as meaningful for our students we began sharing, debating, reading books by the "experts," and recording our views (as a way of understanding the change process) to internalize what it truly meant to adopt the role of a facilitator. This role is needed to ensure students are aware of the value of personal learning strengths, of discovering possibilities, and of networking with others in a community of learners in and beyond the classroom. The education for all is enriched because of the strengths and expertise of everyone.

When problems arose, parents did not point or lay blame. Instead, they wondered if the manner in which an issue was being dealt with was in keeping with our philosophy. Questions were seen in the light of added support. Everyone involved felt ownership. Everyone worked consistently for the sake of children, with the children. Admittedly, we often had to remind ourselves why it was important to give the students a voice. It would have been much easier to just get the job done at a meeting after the students had gone home.

But we didn't give up. And in time the school rooms and hall-ways, the projects and productions, portrayed students demon-strating ownership. (Parents and teachers alike expressed surprise at the innovation and intense concentration of students of all ages as they planned and completed projects.) Parents were encouraged to continue the philosophy at home in a way that would work for their family. The focus of parent/teacher meet-ings facilitated by the principal was about stepping back yet sup-porting the students in their school as well as in their home world.

Staff Meetings

In a community of learners, students feel free to ask questions whenever they need information to complete the task they have set for themselves. Teachers working within this community, building onto one another's experiences, began to view *new ideas* as strategies to be implemented when students demon-strated a need. In our staff meetings, we experienced a new direc-tion — supporting and providing quality time for professional development. Teachers returned to classrooms to facilitate as the children made decisions about the Christmas concerts, the sci-ence project days, or the parent "thank you" teas. The central office news and school business items were left in teachers' boxes for feedback that could be compiled for brief updating at a staff meeting. In this way, we spent less time on administrative issues and more time on professional development issues such as stu-dent evaluations, reporting to parents, how to help students meet their needs in the regular classroom, how to use different teach-ing strategies, school organization and how it might affect the learning of the students, to name a few. Many of these issues, such as the direction "evaluation" must take to support students making decisions about their learning, became debates that were revisited time after time.

The value of each person's voice as an individual and as part of the staff was encouraged as we shared our classrooms with each other and with teachers from other schools, as we prepared talks for each other, and as we organized workshops. Some teachers wrote and published articles in professional magazines.

One principal in particular had a magic that seemed to permeate the building as she encouraged everyone to rise beyond what they thought possible. Invariably another challenge was in the wind whenever we heard her say at the beginning, the middle, or the end of the day, "Try this on for size!"

Research and Theory Become Meaningful

Teachers became energized as they used their own experiences from their classrooms as the motivation to further learning. At one staff meeting some teachers felt their students were not committed and were diverting their energies in negative ways — disrupting the class or being nonproductive or off-task. Someone recommended the book *In the Middle* by Nancie Atwell. In it, the author talks about the importance of the reading and writing process, and student-teacher and student-student dialogue in the learning process. As we explored Atwell's ideas, we discussed with one another what was happening in our classrooms. One teacher commented that her students wanted to know if what she was teaching was really language arts because it was so much fun. Another teacher shared that his students wanted to know if the principal really knew what was going on in their classroom. The feedback continued for weeks.

The teachers were involved with a range of teaching styles[2] and a community of learners as ways to differentiate learning. Atwell's suggestions and strategies were seen as enrichment for the delivery system. Teachers welcomed new approaches as we

---

[2] There are five different teaching styles ranging from totally teacher-directed to totally student-directed. The students are taught the teaching styles and each is given a series of objectives (rather than activities). As soon as a student is old enough to read the objectives — in about grade two or three — he can select the teaching style he prefers. Even earlier grades can be involved in this process. For example, kindergarten and grade-one students may read an objective with the teacher, then make decisions about how to demonstrate their understanding of it.

learned to work smarter. There was never any dispute that teachers are hard workers, but change or new ideas previously viewed as add-on work, were now seen as a meaningful part of the mix.

After a staff meeting, one teacher shared her concern that she often expressed divergent ideas that seemed off-topic to other staff members who were converging with a workable plan. She felt she was different in her way of thinking (she was) and worried that some staff members seemed not to understand her learning style. This was of concern since the focus of the school was an understanding and acceptance of how students learn differently. Were we mirroring what was really going on in our classrooms? The principal reassured her, "We need the rush of ideas and probabilities in order to converge. Decisions are meaningful and workable when we celebrate everyone's learning style and all possibilities." We were coming to know ourselves as learners sharing our experiences and intuitions in a supportive environment.

Professional Development

Professional development extended and grew from informally sharing interesting happenings and concerns from our classrooms to more formal sharing as we read the current research and the practices of master teachers. Many influenced our thinking and inspired us to look differently at our perceived notion of the teaching/learning process. The teaching practices and research became meaningful in the context of the daily experiences with our students. We planned professional times away from our school as a whole staff for purposes that stemmed from our informal and formal sharing.

We invited a consulting facilitator to come to our school. He saw his role as one in which he could facilitate our needs as we saw them in relation to our students' needs. He worked with individuals, groups, and the whole staff. Follow-up work — ongoing discussion and reassessment of what we were doing as teachers and what the students were doing and learning as a result of it —

was insured because the event was staff selected and the activities were preset as part of the total professional development activity. Change was no longer happening in small pockets of the school. As we grew to trust ourselves as learners and to see challenges as opportunities to make a difference, we became role models for what we expected from our students. We understood that together the decisions, in all their diversity, were our responsibility if change was going to happen.

* * *

I have had the opportunity to work with many principals and each school was a nice place to be, but the ones who had the gift of transmitting an energy that encouraged and supported self-directed learning truly had everyone carving a path for life-long learning. They encouraged us to talk of possibilities. They gave us permission to see what was really happening when students demonstrate their understandings of the curriculum and everyday issues by the projects they do. We learned the more students work from objectives, the more likely their learning is meaningful.

Epilogue
WHY DOESN'T MY DOLL CLIMB THE WALL?

...our willingness to rely on truths created outside our experience has cost us the heart and soul of our profession, our belief in ourselves.

– Lorri Neilsen, *A Stone in My Shoe*

I t is important that students have an understanding of how they learn so that they develop a positive self-image. And it is important that the facilitating teacher/role model supports the learning style of each of her students; teachers need to understand how the traditional style of teaching has had a negative effect on the self-esteem of many former students.

MY EXPERIENCE WITH KATHY

I had the privilege of meeting Kathy as she journeyed to understand and trust herself as a mature learner. Her path after high school included studying art, modeling, and teaching figure skating to young children — a job that led to her interest in a career as a teacher. But, she was convinced she would never be accepted into university to study education. "I am only a C student," she explained.

I have spoken with students of all ages with this attitude. They believe their success as a person is equated with marks earned in school rather than in their level of learning. Marks are certainly not the only indication of learning. I believe learning is a combination of experience and memory and may or may not include marks. As Frank Smith (1995, 589) aptly states:

> Learning...usually occurs without our being aware of it, it is long-lasting, and it requires a nurturing environment. It takes place as a result of social relationships (including relationships with the authors of books and with characters in books), and it pivots on personal identification. We learn from the kind of person we see ourselves as being like. Such conditions are annihilated by information — transmission teaching and constant tests.

Kathy spoke to me often about her desire to teach. Each time, I would share another of my convictions about children and learning — convictions that have grown from experience, intuition, reading, and writing. On one occasion, Kathy looked up from her sketching (something I noticed she did continually to make meaning, although she didn't realize it was a strength she could use as a tool to turn Cs into As) and said, "When I was in school, I often felt my answer needed a different question because it was usually not the one the teacher wanted. I was convinced she knew the answer she was going to accept before she asked the question."

She then related the story of her first-grade experience. "I sat at my desk and could never really understand why my doll didn't climb the wall. The teacher had us color a doll that was supposed to climb a stairway built of construction paper, from the floor level, up the wall to the ceiling. Each student's doll would be moved up a step to indicate the completion of reading assignments or tests that required one right answer."

She said her doll was beautiful and different; she had added to the basic shape, giving her long hair, pretty clothes, and eyes that looked excited and alert. She sketched as we spoke and her artistic talent gave a life to the doll that had not been recognized by her elementary teachers.

As we reflected together on her experiences in grade one we chatted about different learning styles and how she demonstrated the ability to think in images and pictures. Her area of strength appeared to be in "spatial intelligence" (Armstrong 1987, 21). I shared what I had read in Armstrong's book, which helps transfer Gardner's theories of multiple intelligences to everyday life (Gardner 1983). As we continued to talk we saw alternative possibilities. Why not try to enter university through a door that would welcome her area of strength? Before long she was planning to share her portfolio with the faculty of art and one morning spilled her work onto the desk of the Dean of Fine Arts. She was immediately accepted into the faculty.

To begin her university course work, she first had to take English. She mustered up her courage and hurried from her day jobs as a receptionist and waitress to discover that she would have to read nine books and write many papers. The professor, it turned out, welcomed her oral ideas in class. She experimented with sketching and imaging to bring the printed words to life. Her first paper came alive as she identified with the characters in the books. She nearly fainted when she received an A. Kathy's second paper became a blur as she worried that she wouldn't be able to live up to an A. Her focus was so scattered she found herself still writing an hour before the paper was due. When she received a C she remarked in earnest, "I really am only a C."

The big question was how to help Kathy to help herself. I asked her if she really listened to her own talk as she excitedly referred to the characters and their lives in the books. Could she let the talk flow onto the page along with her sketches? Could she see her writing as a learning tool rather than as a paper to be handed in for a mark? All of the things my first graders take for granted, as they learn within the support of their community of learners, had not been a part of Kathy's experience. Now came the time to put her risk-taking skills — which she used easily in her skating and art — to work in the world of school. With practice she began to write as she truly moved with the literature and agreed to reach for the thesaurus, dictionaries, and grammar self-help books only when she was ready to add the final "brush strokes" to her papers.

At this writing, Kathy is still pursuing her dream of becoming a teacher. Her grade-one doll is no longer a symbol to compare her with others. She is using her strengths and experiences to become one with her learning.

* * *

The Kathys of the future who — as teachers — will experience a community of learners will help to create more positive evaluation strategies to support children's awareness of the value of personal learning strengths, the excitement of discovering possibilities, and the importance of networking with others. They will come to know that students who share their understandings and discoveries in a community of learners naturally show us the way.

REFERENCES

Andrews, J., and J. Lupart. *The Inclusive Classroom: Educating Exceptional Children*. Scarborough, ON: Nelson Canada, 1993.

Applebee, Arthur. *The Child's Concept of Story*. Chicago: University of Chicago Press, 1978; Midway Reprint edition, 1989.

Armstrong, Thomas. *Seven Kinds of Smart: Identifying and Developing Your Many Intelligences*. New York: Plume, 1993.

___. *In Their Own Way: Discovering and Encouraging Your Child's Personal Learning Style*. Los Angeles: J.P. Tarcher, 1987.

Ashton-Warner, Sylvia. *Teacher.* New York: Simon & Schuster, 1986.

Atwell, Nancie. *In the Middle: Writing, Reading, and Learning with Adolescents*. Upper Montclair, NJ: Boynton/Cook, 1987.

Bach, Richard. *Illusions: The Adventures of a Reluctant Messiah.* New York: Delacorte Press, 1977.

Barnes, Douglas R. *From Communication to Curriculum*. 2nd edition. Portsmouth, NH: Boynton/Cook, 1992.

Barron, Marlene. *I- Laen- To- Raed and- Wrt- The- Wa I- Laen-To-Tak (I Learn To Read and Write the Way I Learn To Talk): A Very First Book About Whole Language*. Katonah, NY: Richard C. Owen, 1990.

Baylor, Byrd. *I'm in Charge of Celebrations*. New York: Scribner's, 1986.

Bloom, Benjamin. *Taxonomy of Educational Objectives: Handbook One, Cognitive Domain*. New York: McKay Publications, 1956.

Boomer, Garth. *Fair Dinkum Teaching and Learning: Reflection on Literacy and Power.* Upper Montclair, NJ: Boynton/Cook, 1985.

Braun, Carl. "Books 'n More Books." *Reflections on Canadian Literacy* Volume 10, Number 4 (1992): 232-234.

Britton, James. *Language and Learning*. 2nd edition. New York: Penguin, 1992.

Bruner, Jerome. *Actual Minds, Possible Worlds*. Cambridge, MA: Harvard University Press, 1986.

Buscaglia, Leo. *Living, Loving, and Learning*. Thorofare, NJ: Charles B. Slack, 1982.

Calkins, Lucy McCormick. *The Art of Teaching Writing*. Portsmouth, NH: Heinemann, 1994.

___. *Living Between the Lines*. Portsmouth, NH: Heinemann, 1991.

___. *Lessons from a Child: On the Teaching and Learning of Writing*. Exeter, NH: Heinemann, 1983.

Chorny, Merron, ed. *Teacher As Researcher*. Published by Language in the Classroom Project, Department of Curriculum and Instruction, University of Calgary, 1988.

Cochrane, Orin, and Donna Cochrane. *Whole Language Evaluation for Classrooms*. Winnipeg, MB: Whole Language Consultants, 1992.

Dewey, John. *Experience and Education*. New York: Macmillan, 1938.

Donaldson, Margaret C. *Children's Minds*. London: Croom Helm, 1978.

Duckworth, Eleanor. *"The Having of Wonderful Ideas" and Other Essays on Teaching and Learning*. New York: Teachers' College Press, 1987.

Dunn, Rita, Kenneth Dunn, and Donald Treffinger. *Bringing Out the Giftedness in Your Child*. Toronto: John Wiley and Sons, 1992.

Egan, Kieran. *Teaching as Story Telling: An Alternative Approach to Teaching and Curriculum in the Elementary School*. Chicago: University of Chicago Press, 1986.

Forester, Anne D., and Margaret Reinhard. *The Teacher's Way*. Winnipeg, MB: Peguis, 1994.

Gardner, Howard. *Creating Minds*. New York: Basic Books, 1993.

___. *The Unschooled Mind: How Children Think and How Schools Should Teach*. New York: Basic Books, 1991.

___. *Frames of Mind: The Theory of Multiple Intelligences*. New York: Basic Books, 1983.

Gentry, J.R. *SPEL....Is a Four-Letter Word*. New York: Scholastic, 1987.

Goodman, Ken. *Phonics Phacts*. Richmond Hill, ON: Scholastic, 1993.

Goswami, Dixie, and Peter R. Stillman. *Reclaiming the Classroom: Teacher Research as an Agency for Change*. Portsmouth, NH: Boyton/Cook, 1987.

Graves, Donald. *Writing: Teachers and Children at Work*. Exeter, NH: Heinemann, 1983.

Green, Anne. "Children Making Sense of Their World Through Writing." *Teaching Today* 111 (6): 12 (May 1985).

Habib, Marlene. "Intuition Secret to Success." *Calgary Herald* (July 29, 1988): B7.

Hare, Jannis. *Sky Puppets*. Unpublished.

Holt, John. *How Children Learn*. Revised. New York: Delta/Seymour Lawrence, 1983.

Lipman, Matthew, Ann Margaret Sharp, and Frederick S. Oscanyan. *Philosophy in the Classroom*. Philadelphia, PA: Temple University Press, 1980.

Lopez, Barry. *Crow and Weasel*. Toronto: Random House, 1990.

Marzollo, Jean. *Close Your Eyes*. New York: Dial Press, 1978.

McConaghy, June, ed. "Reading the World and Reading the Word: An Interview with Paulo Freire." *Teaching and Education Language Arts* 62 (1): 15-21 (January 1985).

McCracken, Marlene, and Robert McCracken. *Reading, Writing and Language*. 2nd edition. Winnipeg, MB: Peguis, 1995.

Moll, C. Luis, ed. *Vygotsky and Education*. New York: Cambridge University Press, 1990.

Nachmanovitch, Stephen. *Free Play: Improvisation in Life and Arts*. 1st edition. Los Angeles: J.P. Tarcher, 1990.

Newman, Judith. *The Craft of Children's Writing*. New York: Scholastic, 1984.

Neilsen, Lorri. *A Stone in My Shoe*. Winnipeg, MB: Peguis, 1994.

Perrone, Vito, ed. *Expanding Student Assessment*. Association for Supervision and Curriculum Development, 1991.

Phenix, Jo, and Doreen Scott-Dunne. *Spelling for Parents*. Markham, ON: Pembroke, 1994.

Pradl, G., and J. Mayher. "Reinvigorating Learning Through Writing." *Educational Leadership* 6-8 (February 1985).

Proust, Marcell. *The Maxims of Marcell Proust*. Edited and translated by Justin Obrien. New York: Columbia University Press, 1948.

Samples, Bob. *OpenMind-WholeMind: Parenting and Teaching Tomorrow's Children Today*. Rolling Hills Estates, CA: Jalmar Press, 1987.

Schechty, P. C. *Schools for the 21st Century: Leadership Imperatives for Educational Reform*. San Francisco: Jossey-Bass, 1991.

Smith, Frank. "Let's Declare Education a Disaster and Get On With Our Lives." *Phi Delta Kappan* (May 1995): 584-590.

___. *To Think*. New York: Teachers' College Press, 1990.

Stomberg, R.D. *The Goose*. N.p., n.d.

Tarasoff, Mary. *A Guide to Children's Spelling Development for Parents and Teachers*. Victoria, BC: Active Learning Institute, 1992.

Tierney, Robert J., Mark A. Carter, and Laura E. Desai. *Portfolio Assessment in the Reading-Writing Classroom*. Norwood, MA: Christopher-Gordon Publishers, 1991.

Upitis, Rena. *Can I Play You My Song?: The Compositions and Invented Notations of Children*. Portsmouth, NH: Heinemann, 1992.

___. *This Too Is Music*. Portsmouth, NH: Heinemann, 1990.

Van Manen, Max. *The Tone of Teaching*. Toronto: Scholastic, 1986.

Villiers, Una. *LUK MUME LUK DADE I KAN RIT*. Richmond Hill, ON: Scholastic-Tab, 1989.

Vitale, Barbara Meister. *Free Flight: Celebrating Your Right Brain.* Rolling Hills Estates, CA: Jalmar Press, 1986.

Vygotsky, L.S. *Mind in Society.* Cambridge, MA: Harvard University Press, 1978.

Wassermann, Selma. *Teaching Elementary Science: Who's Afraid of Spiders?* New York: Harper & Row, 1988.

Wheatley, Margaret J. *Leadership and the New Science: Learning About Organization from an Orderly Universe.* San Francisco: Berrett-Koehler, 1992.

Whitman, Walt. "When I Heard the Learn'd Astronomer." *Leaves of Grass.* Edited by Sculley Bradley and Harold W. Blodgett. New York: Norton, 1973.

THEME CENTER RESOURCES

The following are some suggested readings for the theme center to support students as they shape their learning. Happily, the list is endless.

Allen, Buell, Margaret. "What Measuring Worm Found Out." *Children's Playmate* (May 1979).

Andersen, Hans Christian. *Hans Christian Andersen's Fairytales.* Bristol, UK: Purnell, 1987.

Van Allsburg, Chris. *Just a Dream.* Boston: Houghton Mifflin, 1990.

Asayama, Ejichi. *Dandelions.* Observing Nature series. East Sussex, UK: Wayland Publishers, 1980.

Baylor, Byrd. *Everybody Needs A Rock.* New York: C. Scribner's Sons, 1974.

Booth, David. *Voices on the Wind: Poems for All Seasons.* Selected by David Booth. Toronto: Kids Can Press, 1990.

Bradfield, Roger. *Hello Rock.* Racine, WI: Western Publishing, 1965.

Byars, Betsy. *Go and Hush the Baby.* New York: Viking, 1971.

Carroll, Lewis. *Alice in Wonderland.* White Plains, NY: Peter Pauper, 1984.

"The Dandelion." In *The Canadian Readers,* Book 11. Toronto: T. Nelson & Sons/W. J. Gage & Co., 1927.

Darby, Gene. *What Is a Frog?* London: Benefic Press, 1965.

dePaola, Tomie. *The Quicksand Book.* New York: Holiday House, 1977.

De Rico, Ul. *The Rainbow Goblins.* New York: Thames & Hudson, 1978.

Downie, Mary Alice, and Jillian Hulme Gilliland. *Stones & Cones.* Richmond Hill, ON: Scholastic-TAB, 1984.

Duke, Kate. *Aunt Isabel Tells a Good One.* New York: Dutton Children's Books, 1992.

Evans, Gerrem. *Brendan, Morgan, and the Best Ever Cloud Machine.* Toronto: Annick Press, 1985.

Eyvindson, Peter. *Jen and the Great One.* Winnipeg, MB: Pemmican, 1992.

François, Andre. *Crocodile Tears.* London: Faber & Faber, 1955.

Frame, Lory. "The Trouble with Dandelions." *Highlights for Children* 40 (5): 20-21 (May 1985).

Freeman, Don. *A Rainbow of My Own.* New York: Viking, 1966.

___. *Dandelion.* New York: Viking, 1964.

Froom, Barbara. *The Snakes of Canada.* Toronto: McClelland & Stewart, 1972.

Gackenbach, Dick. *McGoogan Moves the Mighty Rock.* New York: Harper & Row, 1981.

Gerstein, Mordicai. *The Gigantic Baby.* New York: Harper & Row, 1991.

Gunning, Monica. *Not A Copper Penny in Me House: Poems from the Caribbean.* Honesdale, PA: Wordsong Boyds Mills Press, 1993.

Heavilin, Jay. *The Beginning Knowledge Book of Rocks and Gems.* A Rutledge Book. New York: Macmillan, 1964.

Kumin, Maxine, and Anne Sexton. *The Wizard's Tears.* New York: McGraw-Hill, 1975.

Khalsa, Dayal Kaur. *I Want a Dog.* Montreal: Tundra, 1987.

Martin, Bill, Jr. *The Little Squeegy Bug.* New York: Holt, Hinehart & Winston, 1967.

McKee, David. *The Sad Story of Veronica Who Played the Violin.* London: Andersen Press, 1987.

Merriam, Eve. *The Wise Woman and Her Secret.* New York: Simon & Schuster, 1991.

Munsch, Robert. *Show and Tell.* Willowdale, ON: Annick Press, 1991.

Parnall, Peter. *The Rock*. New York: Macmillan, 1991.

Podendorf, Illa. *The True Book of Rock and Minerals*. Chicago: Children's Press, 1958.

Reece, James H. *Lester and Clyde*. Sydney; Auckland: Ashton Scholastic, 1976.

Schubert, Ingrid, and Dieter Schubert. *The Magic Bubble Trip*. New York: Kane/Miller, 1985.

Silverstein, Shel. *The Giving Tree*. New York: Harper & Row, 1964.

Stecher, A., D.F. Wentworth, J.K. Couchman, and J.C. MacBean. *The Dandelion: Examining Your Environment*. Toronto: Holt, Rinehart & Winston, 1976.

Taylor, D. *Family Story Book Reading*. Toronto: Scholastic-TAB, 1986.

Thomson, Ruth. *The Tale of Fergus Frog: A Story of Pond Life*. London: Reader's Digest; Watford, UK: Mothercare, 1982.

Wallace, Ian. *The Sparrow's Song*. Markham, ON: Viking Kestrel, 1986.

Wayman, Joe. *The Colors of My Rainbow*. Carthage, IL: Good Apple, 1978. (book and record)

Wexco, Bonnett, John. *Zoo Books — Bears*. San Diego: Frye & Smith, 1982.

"The Wind and the Sun." In *The Canadian Readers,* Book 11. Toronto: T. Nelson & Sons/ W. J. Gage & Co., 1927.

Wishinsky, Frieda. *Oonga Boonga*. Boston: Little, Brown, 1990.

Yashima, Taro. *Crow Boy*. New York: Viking Press, 1955.

Yoshi. *The Butterfly Hunt*. Saxonville, MA: Picture Book Studio, 1990.

Young, Ed. *Lon Po Po: A Red Riding Hood Story from China*. New York: Philomel, 1989.

BOOKS FOR A FOX THEME

Bisbee, Bonnie. "Clara and the Fox Family." Adapted. *Ranger Rick* (May 1978): 12-13.

Brown, Margaret Wise. *Fox Eyes.* Toronto: Pantheon, 1951.

Burgess, Thorton W. *Reddy Fox.* Toronto: Little Brown and Company, 1964.

Collodi, Carlo. *The Adventures of Pinocchio.* New York: H. Holt, 1986.

Czarnecki, Corinne, and Joyef Czarnecki. *Fox Trot.* Toronto: William Collins Son, 1987.

Dahl, Roald. *Fantastic Mr. Fox.* Toronto: Bantam, 1982

Ets, Marie Hall. *In the Forest.* New York: Scholastic, 1969.

Faith, Jaques. *Kidnap in Willowbank Wood.* London: Heinemann, 1982.

Foster, Janet. *The Wilds of Whip-Poor-Will Farm: True Animal Stories.* Toronto: Greey de Pencier Books, 1982.

___. *Fox Watch.* Toronto: Greey de Pencier Books, 1982.

Harris, Joel C., and Eric Metaxas, comp. *The Story of Brer Rabbit and The Wonderful Tar Baby.* Saxonville, MA: Rabbit Ears Books, 1990.

Hutchins, Pat. *Rosie's Walk.* New York: Macmillan, 1968.

Korschunow, Irina. *The Foundling Fox.* New York: Scholastic, 1982.

Leverich, Kathleen. *The Hungry Fox and the Foxy Duck.* New York: Goodmaster Books, 1978.

MacDonald, David. *Running With the Fox.* London: Unwin Hyman, 1989.

___. *Vulpina, The Story of Fox.* London: Collins, 1980.

McKissak, Patricia. *Flossie and the Fox.* Toronto: Dial Books, 1986.

Mysels, George. *Aesop's Fables in Song.* Delaware Water Gap, PA: Shawnee Press, 1973. (recording)

Mannix, Daniel Pratt, and James Preller. *The Fox and the Hound.* Toronto: Clarke, Irwin, 1967.

Schmidt, Karen. *The Gingerbread Man.* New York: Scholastic, 1978.

Shannon, George. *Dance Away.* New York: Greenwillow Books, 1982.

Switzer, Merebeth. *Red Fox.* Toronto: Grolier, 1986.

Taylor, D. *Family Story Book Reading.* Toronto: Scholastic-TAB, 1986.

Watson, Clyde. *Father Fox's Pennyrhymes.* New York: Scholastic, 1975.